IN SEARCH
OF
SUSAN

A SHEFFIELD FAMILY STORY

PAUL JAMES SHEFFIELD

For permission requests, contact
psheffield@hyperbaricmedicine.com

Cover Photo: The author's birthplace and first home at Old Chicora, Florida

Ordering Information:
This book is print-on-demand through Ingram Sparks. When in publication this book can be purchased through Amazon.com or any physical bookstore using the ISBN.

In Search of Susan: A Sheffield Family Story / Paul James Sheffield.
ISBN 978-0-578-89975-6

TABLE OF CONTENTS

....

Table Of Contents...i
Table Of Images..iii
Preface..v
Dedication...ix
Introduction...xi
Origin and Spelling of the Name Sheffield..1
A Sheffield Family Relationship Chart...3
Additional Information About Sheffield Ancestors..7
   William Sheffield (1700–1764?)..7
   John Sheffield (1728–1790)...7
   Will of John Sheffield..9
   Bryan(t) Sheffield (1781–1847)...12
   Laurens County GA Legal Document 3/10/1813...12
   Seaborn Sheffield (1821–1886)..18
   Sarah Sheffield McCorquodale (1826–c.1880)..25
   Russia Sheffield Sasser (1829–1891)..26
   Prussia Sheffield Timmons (1831–1922)..27
   Delilah Bryant Sheffield Mayes (1835-1900)...27
   Freeman Sheffield (c1832–1881)..28
   Freeman B. Sheffield (May 1859–?)..33
   Susan Delilah Sheffield (1858–1933)...34
   William Aaron Hardy (1854–1928)...36
   Fannie Sheffield English (1885–1961)..38
   Gabriella Sheffield Hall (1888–1914)...39
   William Cebern Norwood "NAUD" Sheffield (1879–1961)..40
   Linnie Sheffield Fowler (1909–2001)...45
   Lyman Sheffield (1900–1943)..46
   Litha Cooley Sheffield (1900–1991)...60
   Fern Lloyd Sheffield, (1920–1993)...65
   Edna Lois Sheffield Lee (1921-1999)..68
   Daniel Leslie Sheffield (1922-1930)...71
   Ruby Sheffield (1923–1925)...71
   Carlos "Cob" Sheffield (1925–1994)...72
   Letha Sheffield Barlow (1927–2018)..75
   Edward "Ed" Sheffield (1930–1983)..77
   Cleveland Sheffield (1931-1995)...79
   Tilmon Sheffield (1933-2009)..81
   Paul James Sheffield (1940–)..84
   Melvin Sheffield (1941–2018)..88

Afterword 91
References 93
Appendix List 95
Appendix A **97**
Early Life in Old Chicora 97
    About The Author By Ray Albritton 105
Appendix B **107**
Sheffield Lineage Before Susan Delilah Sheffield 107
Appendix C **109**
Newspaper Reports of Seaborn Sheffield's Murder in Early County News, Blakely, Georgia
.... 109
Appendix D **111**
Atlanta Constitution Newspaper Report on Seaborn Sheffield's Murder with Editorial
Commentary on His Life 111
    Sheffield's Sins: The End of A Despicable Career 111
Appendix E **119**
Court Records of Those Charged with Seaborn Sheffield's Murder 119
Appendix F **123**
The Civil War Days (1861-1865) and its impact on Freeman Sheffield's family 123
Appendix G **127**
Other Stories of Events in the Author's Life 127
    Story 1: The White Rose 127
    Story 2: The Three Block Journey 129
    Story 3: The Disabled Christian 131
    Story 4: Quick to Judge 132
    Story 5: Value of Faith and Family 134
    Story 6: The Homeless Lady 138
    Story 7: The Lost Car 141
    Story 8: Remembering My Brother Cob 142

TABLE OF IMAGES

···

Susan Delilah Sheffield ix

Preacher William Aaron Hardy 36

Fannie Sheffield English and her mother, Susan Sheffield Hardy.......................38

Lyman and Litha Cooley Sheffield, c1933...46

From left to right: Lois, Litha with baby Edward, Letha (in chair), Lloyd, Leslie, and Carlos Sheffield - 1930 photo in Jackson County Florida)...49

From left to right: Carlos, Edna Lois, baby Tilmon, Litha, Letha, Edward, Lyman, Cleveland, and Lloyd Sheffield 1934 photo at Ft Myers, Florida......................................51

Albritton sharecrop cabin and Sheffield family home, Old Chicora, Florida. 53

Bethlehem Primitive Baptist Church, Old Chicora, Florida established 1871...............55

Litha Cooley Sheffield, c. 1965...60

John Wesley & Mattie Osie Bruner Cooley 61

John and Mattie Osie Cooley in their Hoover Cart...61

Litha and Violet Sheffield, c1985 - Front porch of our house in Old Chicora, Fl..............64

Lloyd, Olen, and Merline Sheffield 65

Edna Lois Sheffield Lee..68

Violet, Johnny, and Carlos Sheffield...72

Joyce and Edward Sheffield..77

Myra Lee and Cleveland Sheffield..79

Tilmon and Glenda Sheffield 81

June and Paul James Sheffield..84

Paul James Sheffield, Colonel, USAF..86

Melvin Sheffield 88

Grandpa John W. Cooley's catch in the creek on our land.................................99

Carlos "Cob" Sheffield in 1989 142

PREFACE

In 1977, I traveled to Glasgow, Scotland to present a scientific paper on my research of problem wounds. My co-author, Doctor Jared M. Dunn, was a deacon in the Church of Latter Day Saints. As we made the 400-mile train ride from London to Glasgow we got off at every church cemetery to search for possible Dunn ancestors. It was an unusual experience for me--which I did not fully appreciate at the time. Within 20 years I would be making a journey in search of my family roots. This effort continued for another 25 years.

When my wife June began researching the history of her mother's family lineage, we discovered that our great, great, great, grandfathers, Bryant Sheffield and James Bush, were pioneers together in Early County, Georgia during the 1820s. It would be 130 years later that her parents moved to Florida, where we met and attended high school together.

Our on-site research had begun in Blakely, Georgia, after my brother Tilmon made a trip through Georgia. A service station attendant had mistaken Tilmon for a look-alike neighbor named Sheffield, and had greeted Tilmon, using the wrong first name. Tilmon visited the attendant's neighbor and learned that several Sheffield families lived near Blakely, Georgia.

Later, my nephew, Olen Sheffield, traveled to Rhode Island to find the tombstones of our ancestors who emigrated (c1630) from Sudbury, England, to Portsmouth, in Colonial America. Sheffield family members then moved from Rhode Island to North Carolina. Our fourth generation in America included Bryan(t) Sheffield who was one of the first white men to settle in Georgia's Indian Territory.

The historical information in this document came from several sources, principally: Courthouse records, newspaper reports, US Census records, tombstone inscriptions, LDS Genealogical Surveys, Joel W. Perry's *Some Pioneer History of Early County 1818-1871* (1968), Canter Brown's *Florida's Peace River Frontier* (1991), and Andrew M. Williams' *A Sheffield Family History* (1995). Some names and birthdates were obtained from family bibles and family members. Photos were obtained from family members.

This research involved many trips to county court houses, libraries, cemeteries, family reunions, and visits with relatives. Today, with our 21st Century internet, we are connected with the valuable research of many genealogists. We are grateful for all of their work and have found additional information on the internet in recent years.

This family story was told with the assistance of three generations. We received treasured photos of our older generations and images that depict the past in West Florida and Central Florida. Family members provided photos that are included with the biographical notes for Litha and Lyman's children. I appreciate the assistance of my wife June, Tilmon Sheffield, Olen Sheffield, Aunt Linnie Sheffield Fowler, Aunt Cleo English Worley, and Suzanne Pack.

As in any research of this type, information may vary among sources. It is also possible that there are some facts inadvertently missing in this record.

DEDICATION

Susan Delilah Sheffield

This family story is dedicated to my great grandmother Susan Delilah Sheffield (1858-1933). She was the daughter of Freeman and Celia Sheffield of Early County, Georgia. Born with a speech impediment, she did not attend school with her siblings but stayed at home with her mother. Family members enjoyed her visits and her cooking.

At age 21, Susan gave birth to my grandfather and named him William Cebern Norwood Sheffield. She called him "Naud." We assume that was her attempt to call her son "Norwood." A family bible lists his birth as September 12, 1879 in Miller County, Georgia. In 1885, his sister Fannie was also born there. In 1888, a third child, Gabriella, was born in Alabama. By 1898, 40-yr-old Susan Sheffield and her three children had moved southward to Holmes County near Bonifay, in west Florida. Our research revealed that Susan was a single mother, and our Sheffield family name is from her maiden name.

In 1898, widowed Preacher William Aaron Hardy married Susan. She lived her last thirty-five years as Mrs. W.A. Hardy. She is buried in the New Home Baptist Church Cemetery in Graceville, Florida, beside her mother.

INTRODUCTION

In our search for Susan, we found that there were several notable Sheffields, and much has been written on the Sheffield family. Freeman's parents, Bryant and Nancy Paine Sheffield were pioneers in Early County, Georgia. Several cousins were politicians, lawyers, and physicians. Freeman's brother, Seaborn, was one of the richest men in West Georgia. Susan's father, Freeman, was absent from most documents. A census record listed Susan's mother, Celia, as head of household and running the farm. Her father's occupation was "none," with the reason given as "fitified." Then, a brief death notice in the *Atlanta Constitution* newspaper indicated he "had one of his fits and fell into the fire."

At the beginning of our search, we could not find anything written about the lineage of Freeman and Celia Sheffield or their daughter Susan.

This story is an attempt to record a bit of the past and to provide information for readers whose ancestors have a connection to our research.

Blank pages have been included in the back of this book for personal notes and to extend a family tree.

ORIGIN AND SPELLING OF THE NAME SHEFFIELD

"Surnames were not used in England and Scotland before the Norman Conquest, and they were first to be found in the Domesday Book...Men often took the name of the most conspicuous natural feature near their residences, such as a moor, or a wood, or a hill..." [Guppy HB. Homes of Family Names in Great Britain, Harrison & Sons, 1890. p15]

During the reign of Edward V (1470-1483), Parliament enacted a statute requiring use of surnames. Surnames were deliberately selected to designate the quality which a particular family believed it possessed (Good, Strong, Wise), to designate the occupation (Baker, Smith, Cook), to designate where they resided (Brook, Lane, Rivers), or taken from plants, fruit, or flowers (Wheat, Peach, Rose).

The name Sheffield is an Anglo Saxon (English) name derived from *Sheaf Field*, which was given to those who worked in the fields. One of the first was Sir Robert Sheffield, who fought with the Christians to recover the Holy Land from Moslems during the medieval Crusades, about 1200-1300 AD [Personal letter from Sir Reginald Sheffield, London, England, 1997]

The spelling of the name was apparently changed at the whim of the clerks who kept parish (county) records.

"*The clerk when making his entries in the parish register, exercised his own judgement, with little regard to the practice of his predecessors, and thus it is that in these old records the principal of variation in a name is very particularly exemplified.*" [Guppy HB, Homes of Family Names in Great Britain, Harrison & Sons, 1890, p16]

Thus different spellings of the name emerged: Shuffield, Shuffill, Shuffild, Sheffel, Shuffel, Sherfiel, Shuffer, Shuffiel, and Sheffield. [Daniel H. Redfearn, Alexander McDonald of New Inverness Georgia and his Descendants, Miami, FL, 1954.]

A SHEFFIELD FAMILY
RELATIONSHIP CHART

In 1995, Andrew M. Williams published a book that traces the Sheffield family lineage from Elisham Sheffield in England. [Andrew M. Williams' *A Sheffield Family History* (1995)].

Elisham Sheffield (1530 - 1549) (my 10th GGfather). Father unknown; b. 1530 in England; m. Mary Allison; d. 1549 in England

Thomas Sheffield (1550 - 1598) (my 9th GG father). Son of Elisham & Mary Sheffield. b. 1550, Sudbury, England; m. wife unknown; d. 1598 in Sudbury, England

Edmund Sheffield (1580 - 1630) (my 8th GG father). Son of Thomas Sheffield; b. 1580 in Sudbury, England; m. 1607 Thamazine in Sudbury, Suffolk, England; d. 1630 in Sudbury, Suffolk, England

Ichabod Sheffield (1630 – 1711) (my 7th GG father). Son of Edmund & Thamazine Sheffield; b. 1630 in Sudbury, Suffolk, England and immigrated to Colonial America. m. 1660 Mary Parker in Newport, Rhode Island, USA; d. 1712 in Newport, Rhode Island, USA

Ichabod Sheffield (1670 - 1736) (my 6th GG father); Son of Ichabod & Mary Parker Sheffield; b. Mar 6, 1670 as the first generation born in Colonial America, Newport, Rhode Island; m. Dec 27, 1694 Elizabeth Manchester, Newport, Rhode Island; d. 1736 Newport, Rhode Island

William Sheffield (1700 – 1764?) (my 5th GG father). Son of Ichabod & Elizabeth Sheffield; b. South Kingston, Rhode Island; m. Mary B. Abbott unknown date/location; d. about 1764 in North Carolina

John Sheffield (1728 - 1790) (my 4th GG father). Son of William & Mary Sheffield; b. Dec 13, 1728; m. Elizabeth West, 1741 and Elizabeth Graddy unknown date/location; d. 1790 in Duplin County, North Carolina

Bryan(t) Sheffield (1781 - 1847) (my 3rd GG father). Son of John & Elizabeth West Sheffield; b. 1781 in Duplin County, NC; m. Nancy Paine, unknown date; d. 1847, Early County, Georgia

Freeman Sheffield (1832 - 1881) (my 2rd GG father). Son of Bryant & Nancy Sheffield; b. about 1832, exact date unknown; m. Celia A. Brown, Jun 29, 1854 in Blakely, Georgia; d. January 11, 1881, Early County, Georgia

Susan Delilah Sheffield (1858 - 1933) (my GG mother) Daughter of Freeman & Celia Sheffield; b. Apr 1858, Early County, Georgia. The father of Susan's children is unknown. In later years, she married William Aaron Hardy, in Holmes County, Florida; d. 1933, in Graceville, Jackson County, Florida

William Cebern Norwood "Naud" Sheffield (1879 - 1961) (my grandfather); Son of Susan Sheffield; b. Sep 12, 1879 in Miller County Georgia; m. Mary Jane Hardy, Jan 29, 1899 in Holmes County, Florida; d. Jan 27, 1961 in Graceville, Jackson County, Florida (Naud's records are signed "W.C. Sheffield".)

Lyman Sheffield (1900 - 1943) (my father); Son of Naud & Mary Jane Sheffield; b. Feb 21, 1900; m. Litha Cooley Aug 24, 1919 in Jackson County, Florida (Marriage license obtained from Dothan, Alabama); d. Oct 24 1943, in Old Chicora, Polk County, Florida

Paul James Sheffield (1940 -) Son of Lyman and Litha Sheffield; b. Mar 26 1940 in Old Chicora region, Hillsborough County, Florida; m. June Campbell, Apr 28, 1961 in Labelle, Florida. Children: James (1962) and Robert (1965)

ADDITIONAL INFORMATION
ABOUT SHEFFIELD ANCESTORS

WILLIAM SHEFFIELD (1700-1764?)

William Sheffield, the son of Ichabod and Elizabeth Manchester Sheffield, is my 5th GG father. He was born in South Kingston, Rhode Island about 1700. He married Mary B. Abbott (unknown date & location). He had five sons, John, Arthur, Isham, Ephraim, and West. He moved to Virginia, and then on to Bertie County, North Carolina. He passed away about 1764 in North Carolina.

JOHN SHEFFIELD (1728-1790)

John Sheffield, the son of William and Mary Abbott Sheffield, is my 4th GG father. He was born in Virginia but moved to Bertie County, NC when he was very young. There he grew up and married Elizabeth West of Bertie County in about 1741. They moved to Duplin County, NC and purchased a 250-acre plantation from Thomas Gray. John was credited with "patriotic service" during the Revolutionary War. Based on his patriotic service, in April 1784, he applied for a land grant of 287.5 acres in Franklin

County, in northeast Georgia. June 10, 1784, he was granted 287.5 acres, not in Franklin County, but on Buffalo Creek, in Washington County, Georgia. [Ref: The DAR Patriot Index]

John Sheffield and Elizabeth West Sheffield had nine children: William (1745), Ephraim (1755), Wright (1758), Isham (1760), Nancy (1766), Louisa (1768), Polly (1770), Catherine (1772), and Tabatha (1774).

Elizabeth West Sheffield died sometime between 1774 and 1779. Following the death of his wife, John Sheffield on Sept 29, 1779, married a widow named Elizabeth Graddy, who had a son from her previous marriage named William Graddy. She granted John Sheffield three more sons: Bryan aka Bryant (1781), Westley West (1788), and Nathan Arthur (1790).

John and Elizabeth West's eldest son, William Sheffield, served in the Revolutionary War during 1782-1783. According to "Georgia Revolutionary War Soldiers Graves," William Sheffield served as a private in Captain Hall's Company of the 10th North Carolina commanded by Col Abraham Shepard from 1782 until 1783. Moving to Georgia soon after the Revolutionary War he was first located in Burke County and then in Bulloch County. He received 750 acres of headright land (land granted to head of the family) in Bulloch County, Georgia where he was buried in 1826. [Ref: War Soldiers' Graves, compiled by H.

Ross Arnold, Jr. & H. Clifton Burnham c1993 by Georgia Society of Sons of the American Revolution.]

When John Sheffield prepared his will, his estate in Duplin, NC included 537.5 acres of land, 3 horses, 15 cows, 4 sheep, 63 hogs, 21 geese, a gun, and assorted farm tools. John Sheffield directed distribution of his property in his will, signed 22 Nov 1790 and recorded Jan 1791. John Sheffield's will identified "Bryan" for "Bryant" and spelled his own name 4 different ways: Shuffill, Shuffild, Sheffel, and Shuffel.

WILL OF JOHN SHEFFIELD

Book A, page 427, Duplin County NC, Jan 1791

In the name of God amen, I John Shuffill of the County of Duplin and State of North Carolina planter being sick and weak in body but of sound and perfect mind and memory and calling into mind the mortality of the body, the shortness of life, and certainty of death, do make and ordain this to be my last will and testament in manner and form following (viz) imprimaturs. First of all I secure my soul into the hands of God who gave it and my body to the dust to be buried at the discretion of my Executor hereafter to be named. And as for such worldly goods as it hath pleased God to bless me with, I dispose of them as followeth.

Item. I give and bequeath to my son Ephraim Shuffild eighty acres of land including the piece he lives on and

9

being part of a tract of two hundred and fifty acres I bought off Thomas Gray and lying on the third and fourth lines of the patent to him and his heirs and assigned forever.

Item. I give to my son William Sheffel, eighty acres of land joining the piece I give to Ephraim including part of the North Carolina Pecoson and lying on the fourth and fifth and given lines of the patent, both pieces, that is to say Ephraim's and Williams to leave with the advice and assistance of my Executor to him, his heirs and assigns forever.

Item. The residue and remainder of my lands together with the plantation I live on I leave to my beloved wife Elizabeth Shuffel during her natural life or widowhood and after her decease or future marriage, my will is that the same, that is, the whole remainder of my lands be sold and divided between my sons Wright Shuffill, Isham Sheffel, Bryan Shuffel, West Shuffel, Arthur Shuffel, and my wife's son William Graddy, share and share alike.

Item. My further will and desire is that my young sorrel mare be sold at six months credit and the money arising from such sale to be divided equally between my daughters Nancy Screws, Louisa Shuffel, Polly Shuffel, Catherine Shuffel, and Tabitha Shuffel, share and share alike, the shares of youngest ones to be kept at interest at her discretion of my Executor until they come of age *or marry. The residue and remainder of my personal estate consisting of stock of every kind, household kitchen and plantation tools of every kind I leave to my said beloved wife Elizabeth during her natural life or widowhood and the raising and schooling my youngest children one the same and after her decease the said to be sold and the money divided between my sons Wright, Isham, Bryan, West, Arthur, my wife's son William Graddy, and my daughters Nancy, Louisa, Polly, Catherine, and Tabitha. But in case of my wife's future marriage, my will is that sale and division immediately commence she having a child part and in that case my Executor to take care of the younger children past in their minority.*

Item. Lastly, I hereby constitute and appoint trusty friend Francis Oliver and Levin Wilkins to execute this last will and testament hereby revoking and disannulling all former wills and declaring this to be my last will and testament.

In witness whereof I have herewith set my hand and seal. Signed, sealed witnessed, published, and declared by the said John Shuffel, as his last will and testament this twenty second day of November one thousand seven hundred and ninety in the presence of Francis Oliver, Levin Wilkins and William Harris. Signed John Shuffel

BRYAN(T) SHEFFIELD (1781–1847)

Bryant Sheffield, the son of John and Elizabeth West Sheffield, is my 3rd GG father. He was born in 1781 in Duplin County, North Carolina. Bryant and his brothers, Isham, Wright, West and Nathan Arthur moved to Laurens County, Georgia soon after its creation in 1809. They had previously acquired property from their father in Duplin County, North Carolina. On March 10, 1813, they sold 293 acres in Duplin County, North Carolina, to their half-brother, William Graddy, and moved to Early County, Georgia.

LAURENS COUNTY GA LEGAL DOCUMENT 3/10/1813

Wright Sheffield, Bryant Sheffield, West Sheffield, and Arthur Sheffield, all of Laurens County, sold to William Graddy, 293 acres in Duplin County NC for $400.00. (Witnesses were Uriah Feagin and Felix Johnson)

Early County, Georgia was created by Act of the Georgia Legislature on December 15, 1818 from the land acquired in a treaty with the Creek Indian Nation. It was named for Peter Early (1773-1817), who was a judge, state senator, governor, and congressman. A pending Georgia land lottery of 1820 appears to be the attraction for the Sheffield families to move to Early County.

"The territory out of which Early County was formed was obtained by General Andrew Jackson from the Indians in 1817 at the conclusion of his march through the Indian country in Southeastern Georgia and Florida. He chastised the Indians in Georgia and pursued them into Florida (though it then belonged to Spain, a neutral power), blew up Fort Gadsden on the Apalachicola River and captured St Marks, when he arrested two men (Englishmen, I believe) and had them tried for furnishing supplies, contraband of war, to the Indians. To their appeal to Gen. Jackson to allow them to have a fair trial, he is reported to have said, 'Yes, gentlemen, you shall have a fair trial, but by the Eternal I will hang you both.' And he did." [Joel W. Perry, Some Pioneer History of Early County, 1818-1871. p 45.]

"The boundaries of Early County was described as commencing 2 3/4 miles east of Flint River on the Indian boundary line and running south to the Florida line, thence with said line to the Chattahoochee River, thence up said river to the Indian boundary line, thence with said line to the place of beginning. This territory was about 60 miles square, and was laid off into 23 districts 12 ½ miles square as near as possible. These districts were subdivided into 400 lots each as near as practicable, 50 chains square, containing 250 acres each, and disposed of to the people of the State by lottery..." [Joel W.

Perry, Some Pioneer History of Early County, 1818-1871. p 45.]

Bryant's brothers, Isham and West Sheffield, moved to Early County in 1817, when there were only 2 other white men in the county. Bryant lived in Pulaski County for a brief interval and then joined his brothers in Early County in about 1820.

"20th of April 1820...The court being unwilling that the people should be hindered from obeying the divine injunction to multiply and replenish the earth, appointed Richard Grimsley, Clerk C.O., to issue marriage licenses until one was regularly elected and commissioned..." [Joel W. Perry, Some Pioneer History of Early County, 1818-1871, p 47.]

Bryant Sheffield married Nancy Paine from South Carolina on October 5, 1820, in Blakely, Early County, Georgia. They had six children: Seaborn (1821), Sarah (1826), Russia (1829), Prussia (1831), Freeman (1832), and Delilah Bryant (1835).

The first Grand Jury was created in Early County on June 5, 1820. Bryant Sheffield was among those selected. In 1825, Bryant was appointed by Inferior Court as one of six commissioners to view the ground and blaze out a road from the Flint River to the Chattahoochee River. Apparently because of disagreement as to its location, Bryant resigned the following year. However, after the road was marked (which passed his house) he was reappointed as one of three commissioners to apportion the lands and appoint overseers to open the road. In 1827, he constructed a grist mill near the road located on Dunlap's Mill Creek, which later became known as Low's Mill. While constructing the mill, his nephew, James Sheffield, son of Wright Sheffield, was killed by falling timbers. [Reference: Joel W. Perry, Difficulties in Getting a New Road, Some Pioneer History of Early County, 1818-1871, pp 115-116.]

"Bryant Sheffield and Miss Nancy Payne, a ward of Richard Grimsley, were married about the same time. He settled within a mile or two of where his son, Seaborn Sheffield, now resides. He subsequently moved to his brother's, Wright Sheffield's place, upon which his son, Seaborn, now lives. (This place is now in the southwest corner of the town of Arlington, and is known at the present day because of the assassination of Seaborn Sheffield there some thirty odd years ago.) His residence was in what is now the field to the left of the road as you go towards Morgan. In 1827 he built the mill now known as Low's Mill in the eastern part of the county, just below Dunlap's, in raising the frame of which a son of Wright Sheffield, named James, was killed by the timbers falling on him. Their children all remain in the county yet. He has been dead many years. His wife survived him several years." [Joel W. Perry, Some First Marriages, Some Pioneer History of Early County, 1818-1871, pp 80-81.]

In 1828, Bryant filed a claim in Early County, Georgia, against the Creek Indians for stealing his cattle and hogs, but there is no indication of the outcome:

"Claim no. 4. Georgia, Early Co. Personally appeared before me, Bryant Sheffield, of said county who being sworn and saith that he has resided in said county about nine years and that he has during the whole of that time kept a considerable stock of hogs and cattle frequently five hundred head and he says that he thinks the Creek Indians have killed or stolen at least twenty head of cattle worth at least five dollars each and he thinks they have killed twenty head of hogs belonging to him worth five dollars each. He further states that in hunting for his cattle and hogs he has frequently seen where both cattle and hogs had been killed which he believes was his and once he says he run off an Indian who had killed one of his hogs which he found and he says that he frequently saw the skins of his hogs which he thinks had been killed by Indians. His cattle and hogs used where no white person resided and the Indians have continued hunting here ever since the country was ceded by them to the whites and have been constantly in the practice of destroying cattle and hogs belonging to the whites. Deponent has no reason for suspecting white persons of having stolen his property. Bryant (his mark x) Sheffield; Sworn to before me this 3rd August 1828. Mansfield Torrance, Special Agent"

Bryant, who could neither read nor write, signed official documents with an "x." During the 1820s and 1830s, Bryant and Nancy acquired 1250 acres of land located between Damascus and Arlington, Georgia. By the time of Bryant's death in 1847, all of it was dispersed to his children, excepting 250 acres (land lot 201 in the Southwest corner of the city of Arlington, Georgia) which was retained by Nancy as her homestead. The 1850 Early County census shows Nancy residing on the property along with two of her children Freeman, age 18, and Delila Bryant, age 15. The 1857 Early County tax records show Nancy Sheffield with 250 acres, holder of 8 slaves, with a total taxable value of $6,659 (equivalent to about $199,000 in 2020). At the same time, Seaborn's taxable assets were valued at $27,549 (equivalent to about $824, 500 in 2020) and Freeman's taxable assets were valued at $2,976 (equivalent to about $89,000 in 2020). By 1859, most of the family property had been acquired by the eldest son, Seaborn.

Early County property records (Book L, p. 517) lists the sale of Nancy's 250-acre plantation (land lot 201 in the 6th district) dated Dec 6, 1858, stating: *the said Nancy Sheffield has departed this life.*" Seaborn, acting as Executor of the Last Will and Testament of Bryant Sheffield, was ordered by court to sell the land to the highest bidder. On January 4, 1859, the land was sold to Allen Gay, Sr for $1505. The same day, Allen Gay, Sr sold it to Seaborn Sheffield for $1505.

Bryant Sheffield passed away October 14, 1847. Nancy survived him almost 11 years, until August 24, 1858. They are buried in adjacent tombs in the Timmons Cemetery, one mile southwest of Arlington, Early County, Georgia, which is on one of the farms that they had owned. During a visit to the property in 1996, the author found that it was still being farmed and the cemetery maintained by Charlie Johnson who was Bryant Sheffield's great-great-grandson. Inscription on Bryant's tombstone: *"TO THE MEMORY OF BRYAN SHEFFIELD WHO DIED OCTOBER 14, 1847, AGED 66 YEARS."* Inscription on Nancy's tombstone: *"TO THE MEMORY OF NANCY, WIFE OF BRYAN SHEFFIELD, BORN JUNE 28TH 1794, DIED AUGUST 24TH, 1858, AGED 64 YEARS, 1 MONTH AND 26 DAYS."*

SEABORN SHEFFIELD (1821–1886)

Seaborn Sheffield, first son of Bryant and Nancy Paine Sheffield, is my 2nd GG uncle. He was born on November 8, 1821 in Early County, Georgia. He became one of the wealthiest plantation owners in southwest Georgia. His 1,885 acres surrounded and included part of Arlington, Georgia. His estate was listed among the elite plantation owners in the area, with a property tax value of $36,926 before the Civil War. (This would be equivalent to about

$990,000 in 2020). The 1860 Early County Slave Schedule revealed that Seaborn was a holder of 24 slaves (p 250, Collections of the Early County Georgia Historical Society, vol 2). Court records from the Civil War era gave the following information about Seaborn. In 1862, Seaborn and his friends provided bond money for a neighbor's daughter in the matter of her illegal cohabitation with Smart, a slave held by LW Lane. They also provided $56,000 bond money for Brinkley Chancy to serve as the Early County Tax Collector in 1862-63. On January 17, 1865, Seaborn was sworn in as Constable of the 854 West District of Early County. [Minutes of the Early County Superior Court, January 12, 1865.]

In 1871, Seaborn's liaison with unattached women of the community, described as a "*disgraceful career with the abandoned women of the neighborhood*" resulted in a charge for fornication, but there is no record showing the outcome of the charge.

Early Superior Court Apr T 1871. The State vs Francis AE Jones, Charge: Fornication; The State vs Seaborn Sheffield, Charge: Fornication. One subpoena issued for John A. Timmons, Mar 9, 1871 for the State. One subpoena issued for Daniel McMillan, Mar 9, 1871 for the State. One subpoena issued for Charles R. Telliaferro, Mar 9, 1871 for the State.

Seaborn Sheffield remained a life-long bachelor, but he had at least three children out of wedlock that he adopted as his own. The 1880 census records him single but lists two children away at school: Eller (age 12) and Nancie (age 14). Seaborn had a biracial son named John Sheffield (JB Sheffield). He kept John at his house with his other children, paid his debts, and defended him against immense social pressures in post-Civil War Georgia.

"*WT Wurchison vs JB Sheffield and Seaborn Sheffield In Early Superior Court, Whereupon it is considered, ordered, and adjudged by the court that the Plff do recover of debts JB Sheffield and Seaborn Sheffield the sum of sixty-one dollars and twenty five cents, principal debt and the sum of five dollars and thirty five cents for interest to Judgment and the further sum of ____dollars for costs of suit. Judgment signed Oct 4, 1883. HC Sheffield, Plffs Atty. John T Clarke, JSCPC.*" [Early Superior Court Minutes Oct 4, 1883, p 145.]

Seaborn was murdered in his home on September 24, 1886 at age 65. At Appendices C and D are newspaper accounts of Seaborn Sheffield's murder. His defense of his black son, John, apparently acquired him a number of enemies. According to the Atlanta Constitution article at Appendix D, the Ku Klux Klan (KKK) sent Seaborn a warning the day before he was murdered. Because he was about to make a will of his property in favor of John, there was speculation that his daughters' husbands may have been involved in the murder. Appendix E has court records pertaining to those charged with Seaborn's murder.

Seaborn Sheffield is buried at Timmons Cemetery near Arlington, Georgia. His tomb is adjacent to his mother, Nancy. Inscribed on his tombstone: *"Seaborn Sheffield, Born Nov 8 1821, Died Sep 24 1886. Gone but not forgotten. Prepare to meet thy God for in such an hour as ye think not, the son of man cometh."* Adjacent to his grave is his daughter, Nancie Bryant Talliafero: *"Nancie Bryant, wife of B.T. Talliafero, Born February 3, 1866, Died January 31, 1887."* Her death, at age 21, occurred as suspicions were mounting about her husband's involvement in the murder of her father. Nancie had married Benjamin T. Taliaferro 3 years previously, on March 9, 1884. Near Seaborn's grave is the tomb of his daughter, Ella Bryant Lawrence: *"Ella Bryant, wife of B.R. Lawrence, Born February 7, 1868, Died April 16, 1887."* Adjacent to Ella Bryant's tomb is her infant daughter's marker: *"Corrie Ella Lawrence, Born April 5, 1887, Died May 18, 1887."* Thus, Ella Bryant passed away 11 days after childbirth, and her infant daughter passed away a month later. Ella had married Benjamin R. Lawrence on June 6, 1886, three months prior to her father's murder. Ella's death occurred three days after her husband was arrested and jailed under indictment for her father's murder.

It is interesting to trace the ownership of Seaborn's estate before and after his death on September 24, 1886. The 1886 Early County tax records show that Seaborn had

1,785 acres (lots 199, 200, 201, 202, 203, 239, 240) that were valued at $5,000 and a total taxable value of $9,288 (an equivalent value of $255,000 in 2020). Ben Lawrence had 300 acres (lots 363, 364) valued at $600, and his total taxable value was listed at $990 (an equivalent value of $27,000 in 2020). B.T. Taliaferro had no land and a total taxable value $182 (an equivalent value of $5,000 in 2020).

Seaborn's cousin, Henry Clay Sheffield, was grandson of Nathan Arthur Sheffield, who was one of Seaborn's uncles. Henry was the lawyer for those accused of Seaborn's murder. Henry had served as the lawyer for other accusers against Seaborn and his son, John, on previous charges. In 1877, Henry C. Sheffield, a prominent lawyer in nearby Colquitt, was elected to the State House of Representatives located in Miller County, Georgia. It is interesting to note that during the period 1882-87, he acquired 2,025 acres of land in Early County, 750 acres of which was acquired around the time of Seaborn's death.

"Whereas, Henry C. Sheffield and Benjamin T. Taliaferro applied to me for Letters of Administration on the estate of Seaborn Sheffield late of said county deceased, these are therefore to cite all persons concerned kindred and creditors to show cause if any they have, within the time prescribed by law, why said letters should not be granted to said applicants. Given under my hand and official signature this the 4th day of October 1886. THOMAS HENDERSON, Ordinary, Early

County." [*Application Letters of Administration, Geor-gia, Early County, October 14, 1886.*]

The 1887 Early County tax records show the estate of Seaborn Sheffield valued at $687 ($75 household, $587 livestock, $25 tools), equivalent to about $19,000 in 2020. Seaborn's estate had been given to the two persons charged with his murder. Ben Taliaferro now had 875 acres (lots 200, 202, 203, 239) and Rufus Lawrence now had 880 acres (lots 199, 201, 240, 242).

In September 1887, BR Lawrence sold some of his land to his lawyer to pay his lawyer fees.

"Benjamin Rufus Lawrence sells to Henry C Sheffield for $1,210 lot 240 in the 6th District: west of Arlington and Damascus road, Except 3 acres to HH Powell, 3 acres (the Wilson Place and 3 acres know as Rollin Colley Place and 6 acres already belonging to HC Sheffield and 4 acres sold as school site to town of Arlington and 1 acre where Hodge Hazle lives, and 4 acres sold to Charles Bostwick said land being conveyed being about 220 acres more or less." [Deed book P, page 12, Early County GA, Sept 20, 1887]

On October 1, 1887, BR Lawrence sold lot 201, Nancy Sheffield's home place (which he had gotten at Seaborn's death) to JW Harrison for $600. That same day, his trial was delayed until the following April, suggesting he might have needed the money to pay his lawyer's fees.

The 1888 tax records show that Lawrence's heirs still had 300 acres, (lots 363, 364); Rufus Lawrence had 250 acres (lot 242); and Ben Taliaferro had 590 acres (lots 239, 202, 203). However, Rufus Lawrence and Ben Taliaferro continued to have difficulties with the law and were defended by lawyer, HC Sheffield. Within two years they had sold or lost all of the property they had acquired from Seaborn.

Rufus Lawrence was sent to prison in October 1887 for carrying a concealed weapon. [Criminal Docket 1883-188_, Early County Superior Court, p 44 #213. Apr T 1887.] In October 1889, Ben Taliaferro was tried and found guilty of fornication and adultery and was jailed to serve time on the chain gang.

"The State of Georgia versus Ben Taliaferro, Early Superior Court special presentation at October Term 1889 for Fornication & Adultery— with verdict of guilty at October Term 1889. Whereupon it is considered and adjudged by the Court that the said Ben Taliaferro be kept at labor in chain gang, on the public works of said County of Early, or on any other work on which the county authorities may lawfully have such misdemeanor convicts worked; And when not so at labor, that he be confined to the common jail of said County—or of such other county wherein he shall be so lawfully worked; such labor and imprisonment to continue twelve months from date---------From which labor and imprisonment

he may at any time, be discharged, on the payment of a fine of seventy five dollars and all costs. Witness my hand and official signature Oct 9th 1889. JH Guerry, JSCPC" [Early Superior Court Minutes, 1887-1892 Oct 9, 1889, p 281-282.]

1889 tax records: Arlington District 1435 was established. Rufus Lawrence and Ben Taliaferro were without property. JW Calhoun owned 3000 acres in Arlington, including all of Ben Taliaferro's lots and some of Rufus Lawrence's (199, 200, 202, 203, and 239) plus 10 other lots. WA Boyett and JC Chandler of Blakely District 1140 now owned lots 240 and 242 that had been acquired from Rufus Lawrence.

SARAH SHEFFIELD MCCORQUODALE (1826– c.1880)

Sarah Sheffield, first daughter of Bryant and Nancy Paine Sheffield, was born in about 1826 in Early County, Georgia. Records are sketchy, but it appears that Sarah might have married Isham Philman in 1842 and William McMillan in 1845. She then married Reuben McCorquodale, but the date is not reported. In 1847, Bryan Sheffield's Will granted the McCorquodales 250 acres (lot 203), which they sold to Seaborn Sheffield (Book L, page 717) and Prussia Timmons (Book L, page 724) on January 4, 1859. A search of the geneology.com website for Reuben

& Sarah McCorquodale, indicated that they moved to Florida and lived at Shell Pond, in Levy Co, FL until their deaths. Sarah died between 1880/1885 and Reuben died between 1894/1896.

[https://www.genealogy.com/forum/surnames/topics/mccorquodale/58/ Reuben & Sarah McCorquodale, Levy Co, FL]

RUSSIA SHEFFIELD SASSER (1829–1891)

Russia Sheffield, the second daughter of Bryant and Nancy Paine Sheffield, was born in Blakely, Georgia on January 1, 1829. She married William Sasser on January 6, 1848 and lived on a 500-acre farm southwest and adjacent to Freeman Sheffield's farm. Their children included: William Duncan (c1853), Mary Ann (c1854), Daniel (c1857), Walter T. (c1860), Margaret (c1862), and Carrie (c1864). The 1860 Early County Slave Schedule indicates that William Sasser was a holder of 5 slaves (p 250, volume 2 Historical Soc book). William and Russia Sheffield Sasser were prominent farmers. Russia Sheffield Sasser passed away November 16, 1891 and she is buried with other members of her family in the Timmons Cemetery, Arlington, Georgia.

PRUSSIA SHEFFIELD TIMMONS (1831–1922)

Prussia Sheffield, third daughter of Bryant and Nancy Paine Sheffield was born in Blakely on March 28, 1831. She married John Aubrey Timmons and owned 1,000 acres of land west of Freeman Sheffield's farm. Their children included: Seaborn Bryant (1852), Jane (c 1853), John (c 1855), Ella (c 1856), Nannie (c 1859), Ellen (c 1861), Delilah (c 1862), and Patsy (c 1867). Prussia is buried with her family in the Timmons Cemetery one mile southwest of Arlington, Georgia, on the farm that she inherited from her father, Bryant Sheffield. During my visit to Blakely in 1997, the land was being farmed and the Timmons Cemetery was maintained by Prussia's great-grandson, Charlie Johnson.

DELILAH BRYANT SHEFFIELD MAYES (1835-1900)

Delilah Bryant Sheffield, fourth daughter of Bryant and Nancy Paine Sheffield, was born December 3, 1835. She married George W. Mayes on December 29, 1853 and owned a 250-acre plantation that was located between the property of her sisters, Prussia Timmons and Russia Sasser. The 1860 census revealed that George and Delilah Mayes had 2 children: Joseph (c1857) and Margaret (c1859). A third child, William B. (c1855), had passed away in 1859. The 1860 Early County Slave Schedule revealed that George Mayes was holder of 4 slaves (p 250, vol 2,

Historical Soc book). George and Delilah are buried in the Timmons Cemetery near Arlington, Georgia. The inscription on George W. Mayes headstone indicates that he was born May 12, 1827 and died June 22, 1862. Beside Mayes headstone is one inscribed: *"Delilah B. McMillan, born December 3, 1835, died April 29, 1900,"* which indicates that Delilah Bryant had remarried to a person named McMillan. A marker for their 4-year-old infant son shows *"William B., son of G.W. and D.B. Mayes, born March 26, 1855, died July 20, 1859."*

FREEMAN SHEFFIELD (C1832–1881)

Freeman Sheffield, second son of Bryant and Nancy Paine Sheffield, is my 2nd GG father. He was born in about 1832. In 1847, Freeman became the senior male in the household at age 15 when his father passed away. He married Celia A. Brown of Georgia (my 2nd GG mother) on June 29, 1854 in Early County GA. They had six children: Elizabeth (1856), Susan Delilah (1858), Freeman B. (1859), Samuel J. (1861) John W. (1863), and Mary (1866).

The first indication of Freeman paying county taxes is the 1854 Early County tax record. He had apparently acquired 250 acres of land from his father (land lot 199 near Arlington, Georgia), but sold it in 1854 to his older brother, Seaborn for $800. He then acquired a 250 acre plantation (land lot 276) located between Damascus and

Arlington, Georgia. In 1855, Freeman deeded the land to LM Wright for $550. The 1856 Early County tax records show Freeman with no land but had $2,663 in taxable assets (equivalent to about $73,800 in 2020). On March 30, 1857, LM Wright deeded the land back to Freeman for $550 (equivalent to about $16,000 in 2020). It appears that this transaction was conducted as a means of Freeman acquiring and settling a loan. In 1858, when their second daughter, Susan Delilah Sheffield, (my GG mother) was born, Freeman's 250 acres were assessed at $550. He had an assessed tax value of $2,976. By 1863, when slaves were freed, he had been a holder of 5 slaves and had an assessed tax value of $6,220 (equivalent to about $128,500 in 2020).

Appendix F is a discussion of the Civil War (1861-1865) and its impact on Freeman Sheffield's family. Hard times during and immediately following the Civil War resulted in many farmers being unable to pay their taxes. Those who had Confederate money could not use it. Seaborn paid the taxes on several nearby properties. Freeman's property taxes for 1867 and 1868 were paid by "Agt for Freeman Sheffield." On May 5, 1868, he deeded 80 acres to his wife, Celia [Early County Deed Book K, p 612 recorded her name as "Sely" Sheffield]. By 1880, Freeman's remaining 170 acres were assessed at $170 and his cash and other assets were valued at $60, for a total tax assessed value of $230. In comparison, Celia (with 80 acres) had a tax assessed value of $195, and Seaborn (with

1,750 acres) had a tax assessed value of $10,655 (a value of $272,000 in 2020).

The 1880 Early County census recorded Freeman Sheffield as being at home with an illness called "fitified." Celia was listed as the farmer. The children were listed as "farmhands." Pareolee, a 4-year-old granddaughter, whom we presume to be Elizabeth's daughter, was also listed on the census.

Freeman passed away as a result of burns from falling in the fireplace on January 11, 1881. Apparently, Freeman was "fitified" for many years before his death. As the first of Bryant and Nancy's children to die, it is likely that Freeman was buried adjacent to his father, Bryant, in the family cemetery. His burial site is unmarked since the tomb was constructed of brick that has collapsed. His brother, Seaborn, is buried adjacent to their mother. Sisters that remained in the Blakely area are buried near their respective husbands, elsewhere in the Timmons Cemetery in Early County, Georgia.

"Burned to Death-- On Thursday of last week Mr. Freeman Sheffield, who lived on his farm, three or four miles from this place, fell in the fire and was so badly burned that he died on the following Tuesday. He had for several years been subject to fits, and had one on him at the time he fell in the fire. He leaves a wife and several children to struggle with the trials of life.--Arlington

Advance." [*Early County News, Blakely GA XXI (29), Jan 14, 1881*]

When Freeman Sheffield passed away, the property was acquired by his wife, Celia (recorded as "Celah") Sheffield (my 2GG mother). Early County census records indicate that Celia could neither read nor write, thus her name was spelled phonetically at the whim of the person doing the recording. Celia was born about 1840, but her age was recorded as "30" on both the 1870 and 1880 census. Her oldest son, Freeman B, was listed as head of household through 1884.

Over the course of 30 years following the Civil War, it appears that there was a religious fervor to "clean up the county of all fornicators and adulterers." Fornication appeared to be the most offensive of crimes at the time since it drew the greatest punishment of spending six months to a year in jail confinement with hard labor on the chain gang or paying the usual fine of $75 plus court costs.

The following court record provides examples of fines: *Trespass $1; cheating and swindling $5; larceny from house $5; larceny from house $50; misdemeanor $25; fornication $75; fornication $75* [Early Superior Court Minutes, 1883-1887, October 15, 1884, p 348.]

In 1884, three years after her husband Freeman's death, Celia Sheffield and a neighbor were charged with fornication: *The State vs Stephen Sasser, Fornication. The State vs Selah Sheffield, Fornication.* [Early Superior Court Minutes, (1883-1887), Apr 15, 1884, p 264]. Punishment for Stephen Sasser and "Celah Sheffield" was 12 months confinement with work on the chain gang, or payment of $75 each plus court costs. [Early Superior Court Minutes, 1883-1887, October 15, 1884, p 348.] A $75 fine in 1884 would be equivalent to about a $2,000 fine in 2020.

Shortly after this indictment, the family apparently split up and moved away from Early County. In 1886, the land taxes for the entire 250 acres previously owned by Celia Sheffield were assessed to AJ Lewis. However, AJ Lewis did not receive title to the land until 1890 when it was deeded to him by JA Hightower for $350 [Deed Book R, p 199]. There is no record of how JA Hightower got the land.

In about 1888, Celia Sheffield, her daughter Susan, and her grandson William Cebern Norwood "Naud," moved to Jackson County, Florida. Until her death in 1913, Celia lived intermittently with her daughter, Susan Sheffield Hardy, and her grandchildren: Naud Sheffield, Fannie Sheffield English, and Gabriella Sheffield Hall. Celia Sheffield is buried beside her daughter, Susan, in the New Home Baptist Church Cemetery at Graceville, Jackson County, Florida. Sale of the land outside the family, minimal records, and fire destruction of the 1890 census have made it difficult to trace Susan's brothers and sisters, Elizabeth, Freeman, Samuel J., John W., and Mary.

FREEMAN B. SHEFFIELD (MAY 1859–?)

We found records for Susan Sheffield's brother, Freeman B., who was born in May 1859, the third child of Freeman and Celia Brown Sheffield. Early County tax records showed him to be the head of the household when his father, Freeman, passed away in 1881. When Celia was charged with fornication and lost the 250-acre farm in 1884, the family scattered. It is fortuitous that a review of homesteaded property revealed that, in 1895, Freeman B. Sheffield homesteaded 40 acres (SE 1/4, S17, R25E, T9N) near Dothan, Alabama, at a place called Mill Creek in the Ashford Town District. Alabama census records for 1900 (Henry County, Cowarts Precinct #20, page 350 B, Line 35), showed 41-year-old Freeman B. and his 30-year-old wife of 11 years, Susan A. (b Dec 1849) residing on the farm. Their children include 9-year-old Ross (b. Mar 1891), 7-year-old Clifford (b. Jul 1892), 6-year-old Henry (b. Jan 1894), 4-year-old Mylow, aka Milow, (b. Aug 1895) and 3-year-old Ida M. (b. Dec 1896). The 1910 census stated that 8 children were born, but there were only 6 living, and 5 were at home at the time. (Ashford Village Precinct, Houston County, AL, page 79b, Line 63) The 1910 census does not list Clifford among children at home, but there is a new daughter, Bessie, age 9. The 1920 census (Ashford Town Beat 10, Page __, line 25) showed all the children had left home except 19-year-old Bessie and a three-month old granddaughter, Hildreth.

SUSAN DELILAH SHEFFIELD (1858–1933)

Susan Delilah Sheffield is my Great Grandmother. She was born in April 1858, the second daughter of Freeman and Celia Brown Sheffield. The 1870 census recorded that she was staying at home while the other children were at school. It is believed that she stayed home to avoid ridicule by other children because of a speech impediment caused by a cleft palate, or "hair lip." [Aunt Linnie Sheffield Fowler, A personal communication, 1996]. At that time, children with cleft palate were sometimes branded as unintelligent because of inability to speak clearly. The 1870 census record is marked that she could not read or write. Since her mother could not read or write, there was apparently little opportunity for Susan to learn to read or write at home.

Susan Delilah Sheffield's first child, William Cebern Norwood "Naud" Sheffield (my Grandfather), was born September 12, 1879, when she was 21 years old. "Naud" could have been a nickname, or it could have come from Susan's pronunciation of "Norwood." The 1880 census shows that Susan had moved away from her father Freeman's home. At age 40, she married Rev. William Aaron Hardy on June 1, 1898. The marriage is recorded in

Holmes County, Florida [LDS Holmes Co, FL marriage record]. At the time of the marriage, Susan had three children: Naud (born September 12, 1879), Fannie (born August 3, 1885), and Gabriella (born July 23, 1888). Census records and family bible entries indicate that Naud and Fannie were born in Georgia (perhaps Miller County), and Gabriella was born in Alabama (perhaps Coffee County). No record could be found of a husband until Susan's marriage to William Aaron Hardy when Susan's children's ages were 19, 13 and 10. This union brought two families together, but it resulted in no more children. Susan Sheffield Hardy passed away in 1933 at age 75. Her grave is in the New Home Baptist Church Cemetery near Graceville (Jackson County) Florida, beside that of her mother, Celia Sheffield.

WILLIAM AARON HARDY (1854–1928)

Preacher William Aaron Hardy

Preacher William Aaron Hardy married my great grandmother Susan D. Sheffield on June 1, 1898. William Aaron Hardy was born on February 6, 1854, to Seenie Ann Hardy (1816-1900) in Sumter County (Americus), Georgia [LDS birth-marriage records]. The 1920 Jackson County census records indicate that he was born in Georgia, as was his mother and father. No record could be found of a husband for Seenie Ann Hardy. The Hardy family genealogy records indicate that she was from Charleston, South Carolina, but went to visit a brother in Alabama to have a baby.

William Aaron Hardy's first marriage was to Sarah Rosetta Spivey (1857-1898) in Barbour County, Alabama where he was a minister in a Primitive Baptist Church. They had eleven children (two of which died as infants). They were born in either Barbour County or in Dale County, Alabama: John James (1879), Mary Jane (1880), Curtis Alexander (1882), Seenie Ann Permelia (1884), Suzianna Elizabeth (1886), Priscilla (1889), Cynthia (1889, died as an infant), Nancy Belle (1891), Marion Franklin (1893), Tildy Melissa (1896), and Daniel Monroe (1897, died as an infant). Prior to 1898, they moved to Jackson County, Florida and homesteaded there. They attended the Bethel Baptist church near Bonifay (Holmes County, Florida). One of Sarah Rosetta's relatives, Preacher Spivey, was the minister. Their farm was about three miles from where my grandfather Naud Sheffield and wife Mary Jane Hardy Sheffield (Sarah Rosetta's daughter) would later homestead.

After Sarah Rosetta Hardy's death, Preacher William Aaron Hardy married my GG Susan D. Sheffield on June 1, 1898 in Holmes County, Florida. Although he lived in Jackson County, it is believed that he chose to get the license in Bonifay (Holmes County) because it was only 10 miles away as compared to the Jackson County courthouse in Marianna, which was 40 miles away. [Aunt Linnie Sheffield Fowler, A personal communication, 1996]. Although the marriage brought their two families together, it brought no more children. Preacher William Aaron Hardy continued to farm until his advanced age and health prevented him from doing so. He passed away on September 1, 1928 at the age of 74. He is buried in the Bethel Baptist Church Cemetery in Esto, Holmes County, Florida, adjacent to his mother, Seenie Ann Hardy (tombstone lists "Ann Hardy") and his first wife, Sarah Rosetta Hardy.

FANNIE SHEFFIELD ENGLISH (1885–1961)

Fannie Sheffield English and her mother, Susan Sheffield Hardy

Fannie Sheffield was born on Aug 3, 1885, the second child of Susan D. Sheffield. No record can be found of her father. She married George English in 1904 in Holmes

County, Florida. They lived north of the Bethel Baptist Church where George English was the minister. They had 6 children: Nettie, Delminer (passed away at 3 months old), Glennie, Cleo, Beatrice, and Velma.

Aunt Cleo English Worley's bible indicates that Fannie Sheffield English was born in Miller County, Georgia. Aunt Cleo recalled that Naud Sheffield and Mary Jane Hardy dated for some time before William Aaron Hardy married Susan Sheffield. She said "Naud was not living with the Sheffield family at the time." [Aunt Cleo English Worley, A Personal Communication, 1996]. Cleo English Worley passed away May 13, 2002 at the age of 88. She is buried at the Glenwood Cemetery in Chipley, Florida.

GABRIELLA SHEFFIELD HALL (1888–1914)

Gabriella Sheffield was born on July 23, 1888, the third child of Susan D. Sheffield. No record can be found of her father. She married James Ervin Hall in 1905. They had 4 children: Sulie, Julie, Leroy, and Troy. Gabriella Sheffield Hall passed away during childbirth in 1914, at the age of 26.

WILLIAM CEBERN NORWOOD "NAUD" SHEFFIELD (1879–1961)

W.C. "Naud" Sheffield is my Grandfather. He was the first child of Susan D. Sheffield, born at an undisclosed location in Miller County, Georgia, September 12, 1879. No record can be found of his father. The bible of his younger sister, Fannie Sheffield English indicates that she was born in Miller County, Georgia. The 1920 Jackson County census indicates that his youngest sister Gabriella Sheffield Hall was born in Alabama. Naud is known to have said that he worked on a farm when he was young. By 1898, GG Susan D. Sheffield and her three children had arrived in Holmes County, near Bonifay, Florida.

Legend has it that when Preacher William Aaron Hardy married Susan D. Sheffield on June 1, 1898, he announced to Naud: "Tomorrow you hold the mules, I'm going to marry your Ma." Naud Sheffield's love for Mary Jane Hardy matured and seven months later, on January 29, 1899, he announced to his stepfather: "It's your turn to hold the mules." According to Naud Sheffield's bible the wedding occurred at "Old Man Butlum's Place in the presence of 'severl.'"

Naud and Mary Jane Hardy Sheffield had 11 children: Lyman (1900), Gaston (1905), Linnie (1909), Rosa Lee (1910), Melton Rex (1913), Leamon (1916), Mary Alice (1918), and four others who died as infants. Naud and Mary Jane attended Bethel Baptist Church near Bonifay, Florida, where Mary Jane's cousin, Preacher Spivey, was the pastor.

According to Aunt Linnie, Mary Jane Hardy Sheffield was known to be a most loving and caring mother. Naud was known as "Papa" to the children, who respected and admired him. Naud Sheffield worked for Mr. Richardson in Holmes County for a year and then homesteaded a farm in Jackson County near Graceville, Florida He was deeded the 40 acres of land (NE 1/4 of SW 1/4 of S33, T6, R13) in 1906. In 1918, he purchased the adjacent 20 acres (S ½ of SE 1/4 of NW 1/4 of S33, T6, R13) for $200 (equivalent to about $3,500 in 2020). The land was located 2 miles east of the Holmes County line and 6 miles south of Graceville, Florida, near Hoover Ditch, which was created in the 1930's to control water levels and prevent flooding of the farms in the area. [Aunt Linnie Sheffield Fowler. A Personal Communication, 1996].

The first finding of W.C. "Naud" Sheffield paying taxes was the 1905 Jackson County tax records. His 40 acre farm was valued at $80, for which he paid $0.48/100 state tax and $1.04/100 county tax. He had 4 cows valued at $25 and other property valued at $25, for a total personal property taxable value of $50. He paid $0.30/100 state tax and $0.65/100 county tax. He also paid $1 for being a male over age 21. Thus, his total tax bill in 1905 was $2.50. By 1928, he had 60 acres valued at $240, for which he paid $2.16/100 state tax, $6.84/100 county tax, a road tax of $3.60, and a special school tax of $2.40. He had a horse and a mule valued at $40, two hogs valued at $5, and household furniture valued at $5; a total personal property taxable value of $50, for which he paid $0.45 state tax, $1.43 county tax, $0.75 road tax, $0.50 special school tax, and $1 for being a male over age 21. Thus, his total value in 1928 was $290 (equivalent to $4,400 in 2020) and his tax burden in 1928 was $30.73 (valued at $471 in 2020).

Naud Sheffield farmed and raised his own meat. He insisted that his family be frugal in order to manage during hard times. (For pick-me ups: "If you get down and low, plant a garden and watch it grow.") Since there was no refrigeration, preservation of meat and vegetables in the hot Florida climate presented a challenge. Some meat was preserved as salt meat. A barrel of water was heated in order to melt the rock salt. It was then cooled before putting in the meat. The meat was placed in the barrel, and then it was pushed down with the barrel lid to keep it in the water. The salted meat would keep all year without refrigeration, but when it was cooked, the salt had to be soaked out.

Some meat was preserved by smoking it. When a hog was butchered, the meat was salted and covered with straw. It was left in the straw for 5-7 days until it dried out. It was taken out and washed to remove the salt. A hole was cut in the meat so it could be suspended in the smokehouse. Freshly cut oak wood was used to smoke the meat. It was smoked until dry to the bone (about a week). It could hang in the smokehouse for a month if the weather was cool. To make the meat last longer, some of the smoked meat was sliced and packed in lard. My sister, Letha Sheffield Barlow, recalls that it was especially good meat and Mary Jane served generous helpings to the children [Letha Sheffield Barlow, A Personal Communication, 1997].

The influenza epidemic in 1917-1919 is reported to have killed more people than were killed during World War I. Everyone was afraid to go out of the house, and sometimes even avoided church. When Mary Jane was pregnant with Mary Alice (1918), her husband Naud and a friend, Bud Wheelis, helped bury the dead. Lyman, my father, was 18 years old at the time and helped by taking the oxcart to check on local farmers. He hauled the dead ones to the funeral home. It was believed that one could ward off influenza with a mixture of turpentine and asafetida (a bad-smelling gum resin from various Asiatic plants of the carrot family used as an antispasmodic), so they always put that concoction in a cloth around their neck before going to remove the dead.

In the 1930's Naud Sheffield had a "Hoover Cart" which consisted of a back seat of a Model T Ford car with a foot board on the bottom and shaves to hook up to a mule.

Since gasoline was expensive, the Hoover Cart was designed to be powered by mule or horse.

Electricity came to the area in 1939, but it took the Rural Electric Association (REA) eight years to prepare the right of way to Naud and Mary Jane Sheffield's house. Electricity did not arrive at the Sheffield home until 1947.

Naud's first wife, Mary Jane, died on August 21, 1940 at age 60. She is buried at New Home Cemetery near Graceville (Jackson County) Florida. I did not have the opportunity to meet her. Naud married Beatrice Carmichael on August 21, 1941.

I recall a visit to Grandpa Naud Sheffield in the late 1940s. At his invitation, Mom, Melvin, and I made the 375-mile bus trip from Brewster, Florida to Graceville, Florida where Grandpa Naud picked us up at the bus depot. He transported us to his home by ox cart, pulled by two oxen. It was a long trip, taking dirt roads and trails across a marsh and crossing a creek to get to the house. When we arrived, it was not a pleasant visit. Grandpa's new wife fussed at him in front of us for bringing guests home. After a few hours we picked up our suitcase and Grandpa returned us to the bus depot. Aunt Linnie recalls "There was a road to the house, but Papa liked to take a trail because it was nearer." [Aunt Linnie Sheffield Fowler, A Personal Communication, 1997]

Grandpa Naud Sheffield died on January 27, 1961 at the age of 82. He is buried at New Home Baptist Church

Cemetery, near Graceville (Jackson County), Florida. The cemetery also contains the graves of his wife, Mary Jane, his mother, Susan Sheffield Hardy, his grandmother, Celia Sheffield, and several descendants.

LINNIE SHEFFIELD FOWLER (1909–2001)

Linnie Sheffield was born the sixth child of Naud and Mary Jane Hardy Sheffield on March 9, 1909 in Jackson County, Florida.

She married Clayton Fowler on July 25, 1926 and had four children: Hubert Fowler, Tommy Fowler, Dorothy Fowler McKnight, and Jean Fowler Weekley. Linnie Fowler resided in Graceville (Jackson County), Florida. She died on April 13, 2001 at age 92. She is buried at New Home Baptist Church Cemetery in Graceville (Jackson County) Florida.

LYMAN SHEFFIELD (1900–1943)

Lyman and Litha Cooley Sheffield, c1933

Lyman and Litha Cooley Sheffield are my father and mother. Lyman was born on February 21, 1900 in Holmes Co, Florida (near Graceville). He was the eldest son of Naud and Mary Jane Hardy Sheffield. Lyman Sheffield and Litha Cooley were neighbors and attended school together. At Beulah School, near Graceville, they attended 1st through 7th grades that were all in one room. They attended Galilee School for the 8th grade. According to Aunt Linnie Fowler, Lyman Sheffield was highly admired by his younger brothers and sisters. He was musically inclined and could play the organ, piano, guitar, and harmonica. He played the harmonica to entertain the children on the long walk to and from school. He taught his sister, Alice, to play the piano so she could play in his quartet. The quartet consisted of neighbors: George Courtney, Brown Carter, Lonnie Wombles, and himself. George Courtney (Aunt Nancy Belle Hardy's husband) was the music teacher who taught Lyman to read and write music. Lyman loved to sing and, as long as he was physically able, he attended any "sing" that was held in his vicinity. In about 1925, he bought a reed organ that had been made in 1850 and moved it into multiple homes that his family occupied. In the 1930s, the door frame of his "new" home in South Florida was too low for the organ to enter so he used an axe to cut off half of the ornately carved top. We later discovered that the organ top was held on by two screws that could be removed with a screwdriver. Apparently, he had no screwdriver at the time, but had an axe nearby.

On August 24, 1919, Lyman Sheffield married Litha Cooley, the eldest daughter of John Wesley Cooley and Mattie Ossie Bruner Cooley. Litha was born on January 26, 1900 in Jackson County, Florida.

When Lyman and Litha married they first lived near Chipley (Jackson County) Florida where their first child, Fern Lloyd (1920) was born. In 1920, they moved into Preacher William Aaron Hardy's house in Jackson County. Preacher Hardy had built a smaller house on the property into which he and his wife, Susan, moved.

Lyman and Litha Sheffield moved into the big house and tended the land. In 1921, Lyman moved the family to a smaller house that his father, Naud, had constructed on his newly acquired 20 acres. There children 2-4 were born: Edna Lois (1921), Leslie (1922), and Ruby (1923).

In the winter of 1925, tragedy struck fourteen-month-old Ruby, who was seated on a box that was equipped with legs to serve as a highchair. While her mother, Litha, went outside to bring in more firewood, the baby overturned the box and fell into the fireplace. She died from burn injuries a few days later, on February 24, 1925.

In 1925, the family moved into Louie Bickers' place in Jackson County, Florida where the fifth child, Carlos "Cob" was born (1925). Lyman purchased a low-speed Model T truck and worked at the blacksmith shop in Graceville, Florida. His sister, Linnie, rode with him into town to go to school, and learned to drive the truck. Aunt Linnie Sheffield Fowler told me: "Litha wasn't as brave as me. One time, she had put all the children in the truck and attempted to drive it. But she misjudged the road, drove into the creek, and never attempted to drive again throughout her life of 91 years." [Aunt Linnie Sheffield Fowler, A Personal Communication, 1997]

In 1927, the family moved into the John Cooley place in Jackson County that belonged to Litha's father. Lyman farmed and had a variety of jobs. There, children 6-9 were born: Letha aka "Aletha" (1927), Edward (1930), Cleveland (1931), and Tilmon (1933).

From left to right: Lois, Litha with baby Edward, Letha (in chair), Lloyd, Leslie, and Carlos Sheffield - 1930 photo in Jackson County Florida)

On the morning of November 3, 1930, tragedy struck the family again as eight-year-old Leslie jumped up from the breakfast table and suddenly collapsed to the floor, dying of unknown causes. There were no prior indications of any medical problems. Aunt Linnie recalls that Leslie and Lloyd had eaten dinner with her on the previous evening and had shown off their new shoes. Leslie had shown no signs of illness at that time. [Linnie Sheffield Fowler, A personal communication, 1997]

As the Great Depression of 1929-1939 heightened in 1933, Lyman, Litha, and their 7 surviving children left

Jackson County in northwest Florida to join a brother, Gaston Sheffield and his wife, Thelma, at Fort Myers, in South Florida. Gaston was working in an orange grove and had encouraged them to move to South Florida, claiming: "Gold grows on trees!" The trip was made in a 1928 Chevrolet car, towing a homemade trailer that contained the family possessions. My sister, Letha, recalls that the wheels of the car had wooden spokes. For a few weeks the family resided at Weaver's Corner in the Palmona Park subdivision of North Fort Myers. One of the residents of Palmona Park was a cousin, Gabriel Hall. The children attended Bayshore School where they received free meals. Letha recalls that she had her first taste of dried venison there. [Letha Sheffield Barlow, A Personal Communication, 1997].

From left to right: Carlos, Edna Lois, baby Tilmon, Litha, Letha, Edward,
Lyman, Cleveland, and Lloyd Sheffield 1934 photo at Ft Myers, Florida

Next move was to the Hellina Orange Grove located three miles west of Alva, Florida, on highway 82 towards LaBelle, Florida. There the family picked oranges and resided in a house provided by the orange grove owner during the winter of 1933-34. Other Sheffield families lived on groves in the area known as the Wallace and Flowery Groves. The children were bused to school at Alva, Florida. Entrance to the school yard was gained by a "stile," which was a set of steps over the fence. In 1934, the family moved to Edison Junction near Fort Myers, which was noted for its railway station and lumber. Litha worked in the local laundry while Lyman sold Rawleigh Healing

Salve and other Rawleigh products (anti-pain pills, cold remedies, and liniment).

In 1935, at the request of Uncle Green Berry Jenkins (who was married to Lyman's Aunt Seenie Ann Permilla Hardy), the Sheffield family moved to Fort Lonesome, located in central Florida. There they would become share-crop farmers with Uncle Green Berry Jenkins and live in an old schoolhouse on Ft Lonesome Road.

Letha Sheffield Barlow recalls her early days at Fort Lonesome and Johnson A. School. "Fort Lonesome had a large sawmill that burned down in the late 1930s. In the front yard of the Fort Lonesome house was a train track with an abandoned set of train wheels that was a source of play. The children attended the rural two-room schoolhouse for grades 1-8, called Johnson A. School. The first room was for first to fourth grade students and the second room was for fifth to eighth grade students." There, Letha was awarded a New Testament for being able to memorize 25 bible verses and a bible for citing 300 bible verses. The bible that she was awarded was signed by her teacher, Lydia Walden, on August 20, 1936. [Letha Sheffield Barlow, A personal communication, 1997]

In 1936, Hillsborough County (Florida) schools in the district were consolidated and renamed "Pinecrest." In 1937, Johnson A. School joined Pinecrest School where the Sheffield children would attend. The school year included the summer because the children were needed at home in the winter to harvest strawberries. School was required until the age of 16, after which it was permissible to quit school to work full-time.

After the 1935-36 strawberry harvest, the Sheffield family moved a few miles away from Fort Lonesome to the Old Chicora region of Central Florida about one mile west of the Hillsborough-Polk County line and about one mile south of the Bethlehem Primitive Baptist Church. Their home was a wooden cabin that was provided by Uncle Arter Albritton, where they share cropped his farm. At that location, Lyman and Litha Sheffield's last two children were born: Paul James (1940) and Melvin (1941). Edna Lois recalls that all the children were sent to spend the night with Mr. and Mrs. Ivy Alderman until the birthing was complete. [Edna Lois Sheffield Lee, A personal communication, 1997].

Albritton sharecrop cabin and Sheffield family home, Old Chicora, Florida.

The crops included strawberries, lima beans, string beans, sweet potatoes, Irish potatoes, squash, collards, tomatoes, turnips, corn, and black-eyed peas. Crops were sold at the farmer's markets at Plant City and Tampa, Florida. Dried corn was taken to the gristmill in Myakka City, Florida where it was ground into grits or corn meal. Baskets of eggs were sold or traded at the Fort Lonesome General Store. Sometimes the sale would be good enough to bring home mullet for a fish-fry, or a round steak that Mom would tenderize by pounding with the edge of a saucer and smother-fry in gravy to serve over grits.

In the winter, the family would go to a cane grinding at Dennis Taylor's place in Old Chicora. A person would push stalks of sugarcane between the two giant wheels. A mule walked in a circle to turn the shaft that rotated the two giant wheels to squeeze the juice from the sugar cane. Out came the sweet cane juice that would be boiled in an open vat and reduced into syrup. The best part of the syrup was the sweet froth, or "skimming" on top. Newcomers would overindulge with the skimming and suffer stomach cramps within a few hours. The old timers (those who had been to at least one other cane squeezing) knew how to pace themselves and avoid the gastric distress. Sometimes the children would be asked to stand in for the mule and turn the shaft.

Bethlehem Primitive Baptist Church, Old Chicora, Florida established 1871

The family attended Bethlehem Primitive Baptist Church where Uncle Green Berry Jenkins was minister. The church had been established in 1871.

As the minister was preaching about the evils of fishing on Sunday, I could look through the wooden slats and see our neighbor drive past with fishing poles in his Model-T Ford truck. How I longed to be fishing!

Lyman Sheffield created a gospel quartet wherever he lived. His quartet would entertain at the Bethlehem Primitive Baptist Church, at all day sings at Myakka City in Manatee County, Florida, or anywhere else a crowd would gather. Ray Albritton was a neighbor who wrote about his experience which was published by the Polk County Historical Association.

"One of our neighbors, Lyman Sheffield, used to have sings at his home and most all of the young people in the community came. Mr. Sheffield had a large family and they all enjoyed singing. He had a rich singing voice and could play his old organ really well. I have some very good memories of him pumping the pedals on the organ and playing Gospel music and all of us gathered around singing. Sometimes there were so many people there that the crowd spilled over into the yard. There were never too many people there for Mr. Sheffield: 'The more the singers, the better the music.'" [Ray Albritton, Recollections of Time Gone By. Bartow FL: Polk County Historical Association, 1997. p98]

During the period 1817-1858, there were three armed conflicts in Florida between US Armed Forces and the Seminoles, a Native American Tribe that was formed in the early 18th century. At the end of the third conflict in 1858, Chief Billy Bowlegs consented to move his tribal members to Oklahoma. Although some remained hidden in the Everglades, this opened the Seminole's desirable land in Polk County for white settlement. Thus, Polk County, Florida which included a segment of Old Chicora, was created in 1861.

In 1941, Lyman Sheffield bought 20 acres of virgin pine and swamp land on the south side of Bethlehem Road in Old Chicora (Polk County) Florida for about $300.00 (equivalent to about $5,300 in 2020). Description of the land is E 1/2 of NE 1/4 of SE 1/4 of Section 6, Township 32, Range 23, Polk County Florida. That property had been homesteaded in the 1880s by John Wesley Gill, who also operated the Old Chicora post office. John Wesley Gill was the son-in-law of Hopkin Padgett, who had homesteaded adjacent property in the 1880s. In 1932, after the death of John Wesley Gill, his widow acquired the land and deeded the property to her daughter, Bessie Mathews. It is not clear whether Bessie Mathews sold the land to Lyman Sheffield, or whether Lyman acquired the land from Polk County by paying the taxes due. Thus, in 1941, Lyman and Litha Sheffield became the fourth owner of the land since Polk County was created for settlement in 1861.

Although Lyman had intended to farm the land, his illness with cancer did not permit it. Litha Sheffield and her children farmed the land. In the 1960s, Litha sold her land to son Carlos "Cob" and daughter-in-law, Violet. In 2020, the farm is still in the family, owned and managed by Carlos Sheffield's son and daughter-in-law, John Naud and Suzie Sheffield.

In 1941, the family moved from the Arter Albritton Place (Old Chicora Region of Hillsborough County) to Clarence and Edith Boyles' Place, which was about 3 miles eastward in the Old Chicora Region of Polk County, Florida. The Boyles' Place was across the dirt road from the 20 acres of land that Lyman had purchased. The move across the county line required the children to change schools from Pinecrest (Hillsborough County) to Brewster (Polk County), Florida. Thus, the children transferred to Brewster School: Carlos (tenth grade), Letha (eighth grade), Edward (fifth grade), Cleveland (fourth grade), Tilmon (second grade), Paul James and Melvin enrolled in 1946 and 1947. Fern Lloyd married Merline Levins (1941) and Edna Lois married William Holbrook (1942) and moved away.

During almost seven years of illness, Lyman Sheffield traveled to many locations for treatment of the cancer that eventually consumed his right nostril, right eye, and metastasized in his brain. In order to help pay his medical bills, in 1940 he borrowed $600 from Uncle Arter Albritton, with whom he was share-crop farming. By 1941, he wore a patch over the right eye. He had cobalt radiation treatments at the Watson Clinic in nearby Lakeland, Florida. Lyman became too sick to farm his newly acquired land. On October 24, 1943, he lost his battle with cancer, leaving my mother, Litha Sheffield, with 7 children at home, ages 2 to 17. His medical bills devastated the family, leaving us destitute. My mother felt responsible because she had squeezed a pimple on his nose where she thought the cancer had started.

I was 3 ½ years old when my father died, so I have little recollection of him. There are three traumatic memories. On one occasion he was seated in the yard when he called for me. I thought he was playing so I playfully ran away and circled a large oak tree. The swat he gave me to my backside broke my heart, for it did not seem to be a fair conclusion for what seemed to me to be a game of hide and seek. A second occasion was on the morning of his death as, through the bedroom door, I could see his still body on the bed and smell the camphor that was used to mask the odor of rotting flesh. To this day, camphor odor is distasteful to me. The third traumatic memory was at his funeral as his body was lowered into the grave.

Lyman Sheffield died on October 24, 1943. He is buried in the Bethlehem Primitive Baptist Church Cemetery in Old Chicora (Hillsborough County), Florida. In 2001, Olen Pasco Sheffield (Fern Lloyd Sheffield's son) was looking at papers in his father's old trunk when he found a newspaper clipping of Lyman Sheffield's death announcement.

LYMAN SHEFFIELD, WAUCHULA, 25 Oct 43

Lyman Sheffield, of Chicora settlement, died at his residence Sunday [Oct 24, 1943]. He is survived by his father, W.C. Sheffield, Graceville; his widow, and two daughters: Mrs. Lois Holbrook, Plant City, and Letha Sheffield, and by seven sons Pfc. Fern L. Sheffield, somewhere overseas; Carlos, Edward, Cleveland, Tillman, James, and Melvin Sheffield; three sisters, Mrs. Clayton Fowler, Mrs. Arthur Fowler, and Mrs. Leland Hicks, Graceville, and three brothers, Melton Rex Shefield,

Lancaster, Penn; Gaston, Ft. Myers, and Pvt. Leamon Sheffield, Camp Blanding.

LITHA COOLEY SHEFFIELD (1900–1991)

Litha Cooley Sheffield, c. 1965

Litha Cooley Sheffield was my mother. She was the eldest daughter of John Wesley Cooley and Mattie Ossie Bruner Cooley. She was born on January 26, 1900 in Jackson County, Florida.

John Wesley & Mattie Osie Bruner Cooley

John and Mattie Osie Cooley in their Hoover Cart.

Litha married Lyman Sheffield on August 24, 1919. They were share-crop farmers who were blessed with a large family to help work the fields: Fern Lloyd (1920), Edna Lois (1921), Daniel Lesley (1922-1930), Ruby (1923-1925), Carlos (1925), Letha (1927), Edward (1930), Cleveland (1931), Tilmon (1933), Paul James (1940), and Melvin (1941).

Two children (Lesley and Ruby) had passed away in their youth. When my father lost his seven-year bout with cancer in 1943, he left my mother with 7 children still at home, ranging in age from 1 to 17. Soon there would be four at home, as the older children dropped out of school and left home to find jobs and make their own way.

There was no electrical service in the farming area until 1955. Lighting was by kerosene lamp and our water was obtained from a well in the yard, which was an open hole in the ground, about 8 feet deep, that was protected by a 5-ft square wooden frame barrier. It had a tree limb mounted overhead with a pulley attached. The water bucket was lowered and raised by a rope that was threaded through the pulley. With little effort, a full bucket of water could be raised from the well and swung onto the wooden shelf where it rested until the water was dumped into another bucket and carried into the house.

The Boyles place where we lived had previously served as the Old Chicora post office. It was constructed like other frontier homes at the time. The walls were made of 4-to-6-inch pine boards positioned vertically in the wall, leaving cracks between the boards. The cracks in the wall were a haven for roaches, palmetto bugs, and silverfish. Insects were killed by throwing hot water up to the ceiling, letting it run down the cracks to the floor. This would both kill and wash the insects from their hiding places. The floor was wooden boards with cracks through which we could sweep dead bugs and any dirt that was tracked in from outside. After killing bugs, the floor would be scrubbed with water and lye soap, leaving a fresh, clean smell in the house.

Water from the well was heated in a kettle outside the house and carried into the house for the debugging procedure. On one occasion, as a child of five, Mom and I were carrying a partially filled washtub of hot water up the steps when I dropped my side of the wash tub and the hot water scalded my legs. Mrs. Edith Galbraith, our closest neighbor, came to the rescue with a mixture of butter, baking soda, and molasses that was soothing to the scald wounds. Although blisters formed on both legs, there was no permanent scarring or deformity.

Mother was a strong matriarch who was determined to provide for the family. When my father passed away, she arranged for a timber company to cut the pine trees that covered the acreage that Dad had bought in Old Chicora. The location is on Bethlehem Road 5 miles southwest of the former town of Brewster, Florida and about 2 miles from the Hillsborough County line. As payment for the timber, the sawmill company provided enough lumber for her to build a house. In 1945, Litha and her children constructed a house and cleared the land for farming, with occasional help from a neighbor.

Litha and Violet Sheffield, c1985 - Front porch of our house in Old Chicora, Fl

The 1940s in Old Chicora were very difficult, but character building as the children took on adult roles early. Mom's frugality, determination, and loyalty to us kept our family intact during those hard times. She threw nothing away. For many years, Dad's overalls hung on the bedroom closet door, serving as a daily reminder that we must make it without him. We wore hand-me-down overalls with patches at the knees. Shirts were made from feed sacks and underwear was made from flour sacks. Scraps of cloth were sewn into quilts.

The 1950s were a little less difficult in Old Chicora as electrical power was installed in the neighborhood and

Mom got a job washing dishes at the Brewster Elementary and Junior High School lunchroom. A description of Life in Old Chicora is at Attachment A. [Sheffield, PJ. Early Life in Old Chicora, Polk County Historical Quarterly, Vol 21, No 1, June 1994, pp 4-5.]

After all the children had grown up and moved away from home, my mother continued to live in the farm house that she had built for another 25 years, until she got too feeble and entered a nursing home. Litha Cooley Sheffield died on June 22, 1991, at age 91. She is buried adjacent to Lyman Sheffield at the Bethlehem Primitive Baptist Church Cemetery in Old Chicora (Hillsborough County), Florida.

FERN LLOYD SHEFFIELD, (1920–1993)

Lloyd, Olen, and Merline Sheffield

Fern Lloyd Sheffield, the first child of Lyman and Litha Sheffield, was born on February 26, 1920 in Jackson County, Florida. He was 23 years old when his father died. In 1941, he married Merline Levins and soon thereafter left home to join a Civilian Conservation Corps (CCC) Program in California, where he worked on the Yosemite Park Construction Project.

On July 7, 1942, three days after the birth of his eldest son, Olen Pascoe Sheffield, he was drafted into the US Army. He served as a communications specialist (radioman) in the Pacific Theater during WWII.

In 2001, Lloyd's diary that he had written during the war was discovered in a family trunk by his son, Olen.

Lloyd's diary had the following entries:

7-10-42 Camp Blanding Fla, Induction

7-11-42 Ft McClellan Ala, Basic

7-16-42 Ft McClellan Ala, Actual start Basic

9-16-42 Left McClellan by train for Ft Ord, Calif

10-1-42 Time sailed 11:45. Port of debarkation:
     Auckland, New Zealand

10-22-42 Arrived 5:00 pm; assigned 103 Inf, 1st BN HQ
     Address: Fern L. Sheffield 34209464
     1st BN/AQ Co 103 Inf, APO #43
     c/o Postmaster, San Francisco, California

2-16-43 0600. Guadalcanal. Ship John Penn. 5 ships in
     convoy. Under fire 12 hours. US flag raised Feb
     (around) 19th 1943

2-21-43 0630. Russell Islands. Destroyer (?).

4 ships in convoy. No fire. All secure Feb 23, 43.
6-30-43 0810. New Georgia. LST (?). Unknown # other
ships, Destroyers. Under fire 37 days.
Had control of island Aug 6, 43.
7-15-44 0930. USS David C. Shanks ATS. 27 other ships in convoy.
Under fire 45 days, Aug 31 44.
7-22-44 Malaria, 8 days (Medical officer Capt Harr)
? Medical treatment for tonsils, 3 weeks

No entries were made in the diary from August 6, 1943 to July 15, 1944. During that interval of time, Lloyd and other radiomen were sent ashore to man a forward observation post on one of the New Georgia Islands in the South Pacific. Their task was to report enemy ship activities. They were abandoned there for a year. Some of his companions died of starvation and Lloyd was "skin and bones" on recovery. He rarely spoke of his war experience but on one occasion mentioned that his primary source of food was coconuts, birds, and rodents.

After his return from military service, Lloyd settled in Bradley Junction, Florida and worked in the Kirkland Grocery Store as Meat Department Manager.

Lloyd and Merline Levins Sheffield had six children: Olen Pascoe (1942), Harry Gene (1946), Carolyn (1948), Charles Edward (1951-1957), Linda Sue (1952), and David (1957).

Lloyd always had a garden, loved to fish, and could play "blues" on a harmonica so sad that you wanted to cry. He retired in 1985 and succumbed to cancer on April 14, 1993.

Fern Lloyd Sheffield is buried at the Willow Oak Cemetery, Mulberry (Polk County) Florida beside his wife, Merline.

EDNA LOIS SHEFFIELD LEE (1921-1999)

Edna Lois Sheffield Lee

Edna Lois Sheffield, the second child of Lyman and Litha Sheffield, was born September 17, 1921 in Jackson County, Florida. Her family called her Lois. She was 22 years old when her father died. She graduated from Pinecrest High School to become the first high school graduate in our family. She attended secretarial school in 1942 but quit one week before graduation to marry a transient soldier, William Holbrook. The marriage was later annulled. She then wed Earl W. Duncan in 1944 with whom she had a daughter, Mary Jane Duncan (1945-1953). That marriage ended in divorce. In 1948, she married Daniel Lee with whom she had 5 children: Maybelle (1950), Lyman (1954), Leamon (1954), Thomas (1955), and Robert Edward (1957). Lyman and Leamon were twins who got lots of attention at our family get-togethers.

Daniel "Dan" Lee, and his brother Woodrow Lee, served in the European Theater of Operations during World War II. Dan entered the Army in 1943, trained at Camp Blanding, Florida. He served in the 124th Infantry in North Africa against Rommel's German troops. He entered Italy at Anzio Beach where he was injured and received the Purple Heart Medal. His unit advanced through Italy and he was attached to the French Army where he fought at Colmar Pocket, France. A second war injury earned an Oak Leaf Cluster to the Purple Heart Medal. The French Army decorated him with the Croix de Guerre for bravery in action. Unable to correct shrapnel wounds to his back, the Army medically retired him.

Woodrow Lee entered the Army in 1943 as a military policeman. He went to England, crossed the English Channel, landed at Utah Beach, France, and followed General George Patton as he crossed France and Germany. According to Woodrow, "It was a long way

behind General Patton because he moved so fast."
[Woodrow Lee, A Personal Communication, Oct. 1997].

One of my early memories of Dan and Lois Sheffield Lee was a visit to their home at Chokoloskee Island located on the Florida SW Gulf Coast, where they were commercial fishermen. Dan met us with his small fishing boat at Everglade City, Florida, which is about 35 miles south of Naples, Florida. We rode the boat for about 4 miles before arriving at the island. Saltwater fishing was new to me, and I was amazed at the size of the sheepshead fish and groupers that we caught on cane poles with steel lines. Mary Jane Duncan, Lois's 7-year-old daughter by a previous marriage, was sick with an earache at the time, and she died shortly after our visit. She is buried next to Litha and Lyman Sheffield at the Bethlehem Primitive Baptist Church Cemetery in Old Chicora (Hillsborough County), Florida.

In the early 1950s, Dan and Lois Lee's family moved to Alva, Florida, about 20 miles east of Ft Myers, Florida. We visited them several times. It was an 85-mile drive through the marshlands between Fort Meade and Alva, which we always seemed to drive at night. On one trip our car broke down midway and, after hours of fighting mosquitoes, a rancher rescued us and towed us to Alva. On another occasion, Dan invited me to play guitar music with him at church. He was an excellent guitarist and we had played together several times.

In the early 1960s, the Lee family moved to Fort Meade, Florida. Dan's brother, Woodrow, was a life-long bachelor and was a boarder at their Ft. Meade home for many years. Dan tried his hand at several jobs, which included truck driving, but his back pain was too severe, and he finally totally retired until his death on March 28, 1990. Lois resided in Fort Meade until pancreatic cancer caused her death on June 17, 1999. Daniel and Edna Lois Lee are buried at the Evergreen Cemetery in Fort Meade (Polk County), Florida.

DANIEL LESLIE SHEFFIELD (1922-1930)

Daniel Leslie Sheffield, the third child of Lyman and Litha Sheffield, was born on November 7, 1922 in Jackson County, Florida. He was called Leslie. He was known as an excellent student. Although he had not reported being ill, he collapsed at the breakfast table and died of an undetermined cause on November 3, 1930, four days before his eighth birthday. Daniel Leslie Sheffield is buried at New Home Baptist Church Cemetery near Graceville (Jackson County), Florida.

RUBY SHEFFIELD (1923–1925)

Ruby Sheffield, the fourth child of Lyman and Litha Sheffield, was born on December 17, 1923 in Jackson

County, Florida. When she was fourteen months old, her highchair overturned while her mother was outside bringing in firewood. She fell into the fireplace and died of fatal burns on February 24, 1925. Ruby Sheffield is buried beside her brother Daniel Leslie Sheffield at New Home Baptist Church Cemetery near Graceville (Jackson County), Florida.

CARLOS "COB" SHEFFIELD (1925–1994)

Violet, Johnny, and Carlos Sheffield

Carlos Sheffield, the fifth child of Lyman and Litha Sheffield, was born on September 15, 1925 in Jackson County, Florida. When our father died in 1943, Carlos aka

"Cob" was 18 years old and he was left as the senior male family member, since his older brother, Fern Lloyd, was deployed overseas in the Army. Cob dropped out of school to work fulltime at a lumber mill near Brewster, Florida. In 1945, he and his mother were the primary builders of the family home on the land that his father had bought. On February 2, 1946, Cob married Violet Lucille Rowell and they had one child, John Naud Sheffield (1952).

In the 1950s Cob opened his business, Sheffield Plumbing & Electric, in Ft Meade, Florida. During the 1950s-70s, each of us Sheffield brothers would be briefly brought in to assist him in the plumbing and electrical business and learn the trade. When Cob retired in the 1970s, Sheffield Plumbing & Electric was managed by his son, John Naud Sheffield.

In the 1950s, Cob and Violet bought 20 acres of land in Old Chicora (adjacent to the Litha Sheffield home place) and shortly thereafter Litha Sheffield sold her home place to Cob which resulted in his 40-acre spread. As next-door neighbors, Cob and Violet provided our mother great assistance during her time as a single parent and as she aged.

In my youth, Cob served as my surrogate father. One of my early memories of my big brother was when I was about four. He brought home a green Ford Coupe, with the rumble seat in the back, and one of the prettiest women I had ever seen. He and Violet let me ride in the rumble seat that night and took me to my first football game in Fort Meade, Florida. Then, when I became old enough to date, he loaned me his truck with "Sheffield Plumbing & Electric" written on the side. He taught me a valuable lesson: If you want to know whether a girl really likes you, just pick her up in a plumbing truck. I could always depend on him to be there for me when I needed help with my 4-H projects, or with tough chores around the farm, or acquiring spending money, or loan of a car, or advice about dating.

Cob was an excellent musician. He entertained with the guitar, mandolin, or fiddle. He taught me how to play the guitar. When I was in high school, he also helped Melvin and me set up our Country and Western Band which entertained at the Mulberry High School assemblies. Our band also entertained at the 1957 Florida State Fair in Tampa, Florida.

Cob and Violet owned several rental properties in Ft Meade including the building that housed the Broadway Restaurant. On August 25, 1994, Cob was in the Broadway Restaurant helping close for the day when the manager's estranged husband entered and started shooting a pistol. Cob and workers scurried for cover outside the building, but he was unable to escape. The killer followed Cob outside, shot him execution style, and then ran back into the restaurant. Police surrounded the building and in the ensuing shoot-out, the gunman was fatally wounded.

On Cob's death, John and his wife Suzie acquired the Sheffield Plumbing and Electric business and the orange groves in Old Chicora. Carlos Sheffield is buried at the Bethlehem Primitive Baptist Church Cemetery, Old Chicora (Hillsborough County), Florida.

LETHA SHEFFIELD BARLOW (1927–2018)

Letha Sheffield Barlow

Letha Sheffield, aka Aletha Sheffield, the sixth child of Lyman and Litha Sheffield, was born on October 26, 1927 in Jackson County, Florida. When she was four, the family tried to escape the Great Depression by moving from Jackson County in Northwest Florida to Ft Myers in South Florida. Two years later they moved to Old Chicora, Florida. She was 16 years old when her father died. Letha was an excellent student with a great memory. In the third grade, she was awarded a New Testament for memorizing 25 bible verses and awarded a Bible for citing 300 bible verses.

After high school, she worked briefly in Plant City, Florida. She married Obie Lee Barlow in 1946 and had two daughters, Barbara Ann (1947) and Betty Sue (1948). Obie Lee worked as a machinist and trucker at American Cyanamid Company in Brewster, Florida.

Letha was an accomplished seamstress and handcrafter. Her crochet work was delicate and beautiful, with the pineapple pattern being her favorite.

At age 45, Letha moved to Pensacola, Florida where she took classes at Pensacola Junior College. She worked in the Archive Records Department of the Courthouse until retirement.

Following a decline in health, she resided in a nursing home near her daughters in Baton Rouge, Louisiana. On June 21, 2018 she died in her sleep with her daughters at her bedside. Letha Sheffield Barlow is buried at New Home Baptist Church Cemetery, in Graceville (Jackson County), Florida.

Joyce and Edward Sheffield

Edward "Ed" Sheffield, the seventh child of Lyman and Litha Sheffield, was born on January 4, 1930 in Jackson County, Florida. He was 13 years old when his father died. When he was sixteen, he "quituated" high school and left home to find work in the gladiola fields in Ft Myers, Florida. At age eighteen he moved to Mishawaka, Indiana for a manufacturing job. There he met and married Joyce Weaver of Linton, Indiana in 1949, and the union produced one child, Edward "Eddie" Lyman (1950). Ed had several jobs in Indiana: at the Ball Band Rubber Company (making Red Ball shoes); at Don Moore (undercoating cars); at RCA (Supervisor); and at General Electric, where an industrial accident amputated his right index finger. When his finger was surgically reapplied, the nerves were not attached, leaving him with the inability to bend the finger, so it always pointed out into space. When he played the guitar, he was always pointing at the audience. Sometimes the finger would slip off his table knife and flick food from his plate. When I asked him to pass the biscuits, he would stick his finger through it and when I received the biscuit, it looked like a donut.

In 1956, Ed and his family returned to Ft Meade, Florida, where he worked at Sheffield Plumbing and Electric for 3 years. He also attended night school at Fort Meade High School and received his high school diploma "with straight A's" at age 29. That year, he was called to the ministry. He and volunteers constructed the First Church of God in La Belle, Florida where he was pastor for 2 years. In 1961, he returned to Linton, Indiana where he and volunteers built First Church of God in Linton, and he became pastor. In 1961, he also attended a beauty school in Sullivan, Indiana and set up Mr. Ed Hair Fashions where he, Joyce, and several employees were hair stylists.

In the early 1970s, Ed again returned to Ft Meade, Florida where he formed a home construction partnership with Frank Weiser, a building contractor. Many of the homes in Fort Meade were constructed or repaired by Ed and his partners. In 1974, he became pastor of the First Church of God on South Perry Ave in Ft Meade, Florida where he served 7 years prior to his death from cancer. Although he was a much-beloved pastor of 3 churches, he remained fully employed in construction and repairs.

Edward's greatest love was his ministry. As a much beloved Church of God preacher, he was noted for his kindness and consideration of others. On each visit to shut-in members of his congregation, he would take his toolkit and make gratis repairs at their house. Sermons were filled with hope and sprinkled with humor. On July 18, 1983, at age 53, Ed died from cancer that started as a lump on his spine. He is buried at Evergreen Cemetery in Fort Meade (Polk County), Florida.

CLEVELAND SHEFFIELD (1931-1995)

Myra Lee and Cleveland Sheffield

Cleveland Sheffield, the eighth child of Lyman and Litha Sheffield, was born November 15, 1931 in Jackson County, Florida. He was 12 years old when his father died. He quit high school to do farm work, harvesting truck crops and strawberries. In 1951, he married Myra Lee Albritton and set up residence in Bradley, Florida. The union produced two daughters, Myra Annette (1952) and Karen Jane (1955). He was a tractor operator for a local farmer, worked as an automobile mechanic, and eventually acquired a job at Swift & Company in Fort Meade, Florida, where he was a Switchman on trains that hauled phosphate. In 1961, a gasoline truck collided with his train and left him with badly burned face and hands. After a year of recovery, he returned to Swift & Company as a maintenance man. Although he had limited use of his hands, Cleveland never lost his spirit or his strong work ethic. Swift & Company managers regarded him so highly that, when the Company sold and closed, they continued to retain him--with salary--until his eventual retirement.

Cleveland was diagnosed with bladder cancer and died on December 14, 1995 at age 64. Leukemia caused Myra's death on May 10, 1999. Cleveland and Myra are buried at the Evergreen Cemetery in Fort Meade, (Polk County), Florida.

Tilmon and Glenda Sheffield

Tilmon Sheffield, the ninth child of Lyman and Litha Sheffield, was born on September 5, 1933 in Chipley (Jackson County), Florida. He was an infant when the family moved to South Florida. He was 10 years old when his father died. At an early age he learned the art of farming with a mule and plow in Old Chicora, Florida. In the eighth grade, he was May Day King at the Brewster Junior High School May Day Celebration.

At age 18, he quit high school to join the Army to serve during the Korean War. His first Army job was in food service. He then cross-trained to microwave communications and was rapidly promoted to First

Sergeant. He served several stateside and overseas tours including Germany, Japan, South Korea, Thailand, and Vietnam. He had combat tours in both South Korea and in Vietnam.

In 1958, Tilmon married Glenda Karen McNeil and they had three children: Edwin Curtis (1959), Donna Laverne (1961), and Malcolm Dale (1965). Except for the two combat tours of duty in South Korea and Vietnam, his family was able to accompany him during his tours of duty.

In 1971, Tilmon retired in the grade of Master Sergeant after twenty years of military service. He returned to Old Chicora, Florida where he specialized in plumbing, electrical, and carpentry repairs of local homes. Then, for over twenty years, he was an electronics technician at the phosphate mines at Brewster, Florida until his second retirement in 1998.

As a hobby, he had an orange grove, pecan orchard, livestock, gardened, produced honey, and made syrup. He owned the only operable cane squeezer in the county. Then, he and Glenda moved to a farm near Glennville, Georgia. His favorite pastime was giving away his pecans, fruit, vegetables, and honey to his neighbors and soldiers at nearby Ft Stewart, Georgia. Each Thanksgiving he sent me Vidalia onion sets and later we would compare notes on whose onions grew the largest. For 15 years, he always had the largest onion. I think his secret was that Glenda was actually the person tending his onions.

Over the years, many stories about "Mean Tilmon" and life in Old Chicora have sneaked into my lectures to keep the audience awake. So, when Tilmon and Glenda went to Washington DC in 1992 to attend my Air Force retirement ceremony, the people spread the news "Mean Tilmon is here!" They all wanted to meet Mean Tilmon.

In 2008, Tilmon and Glenda celebrated their 50th wedding anniversary. He was a devout family man; he adored Glenda, Chris, Donna, Malcolm, his 9 grandchildren and his 3 great grandchildren.

Tilmon Sheffield lost his struggle with lung cancer on Sep 2, 2009. He is buried at the Bethlehem Primitive Baptist Church Cemetery in Old Chicora (Hillsborough County), Florida.

June and Paul James Sheffield

Paul James Sheffield, the tenth child of Lyman and Litha Sheffield, was born March 26, 1940 in Old Chicora Region of Hillsborough County near Brewster, Florida. He was 3 ½ years old when his father died. He attended Brewster Elementary School, Brewster Junior High School, and Mulberry High School in Polk County, Florida. As a member of the 4-H and Future Farmers of America (FFA) Clubs, he showed beef and dairy cattle at County and State Fairs. With the assistance of older brother, Carlos, Paul and Melvin had a Country and Western Band that entertained at high school assemblies. The band also entertained at the 1957 Florida State Fair in

Tampa. Paul played the guitar and harmonica, Melvin played the mandolin and banjo, and two classmates played the fiddle and the washtub bass.

In 1961 Paul married June Campbell. They have two sons, James (1962) and Robert (1965).

In 1962, Paul graduated from the University of Florida with a BS degree in chemistry. After college, he joined the Air Force for a 30-year career as an Aerospace Physiologist, and served in several positions in hospital administration, aircrew training, pressure suit support of high-altitude flight, and hyperbaric medicine. While in the Air Force, he earned MS and PhD degrees in Human Physiology at the University of Southern California.

Paul entered the US Air Force in 1962 and became Medical Squadron Commander at Langley Air Force Base, Virginia. In 1965, he began his Air Force Aerospace Physiology career. Primary duties were aircrew training, research, and hyperbaric medicine. He was a member of the original team that established the USAF Hyperbaric Medicine Center at Brooks Air Force Base, Texas in 1974. His scientific studies helped create the scientific basis for a new medical treatment called "Hyperbaric Oxygen Therapy" or Hyperbaric Medicine. During 1984-1988, he was Director of the US Air Force U-2 and SR-71 Pressure Suit Depot where he had the rare privilege of taking a flight in the TR-1 aircraft (two seat version of the U-2 aircraft) to above 70,000 ft, which is twice the altitude of commercial aircraft flights. Paul states, "My most profound memory is that I could look down and see the earth's curvature and look up at the black sky with stars shining in the middle of the day.

Paul James Sheffield, Colonel, USAF

Paul became Chief of Aerospace Physiology at the Office of the Air Force Surgeon General in Washington DC, and retired in 1992 in the grade of Colonel, after 30 years of military service.

In 1992, he became Director of Research & Education for International ATMO, a provider of Wound Care and Hyperbaric Medicine services. He became ATMO President in 2000, sharing ownership of the corporation with his two sons, James and Robert.

As a recreational diver he taught diving medicine courses at several locations in the Caribbean. He is a frequent lecturer in hyperbaric physiology, safety, and diving medicine. He has authored 145+ scientific publications that include 14 book chapters, and he co-edited five books [Wound Care Practice (Best Publ., 2004, 2007); Wound Care Certification Study Guide (Best Publ., 2011, 2016); and Textbook of Chronic Wound Care (Best Publ., 2018].

Paul James Sheffield was inducted into the 1994 Polk County Public Schools Hall of Fame and the 1995 Mulberry High School Hall of Fame. He has received several awards for his professional contributions to aerospace medicine and to hyperbaric medicine. In 2009, the Gulf Coast Chapter of the Undersea and hyperbaric Medical Society created the Paul James Sheffield Education Award to be presented annually to a person who made significant contributions to science and education in undersea and hyperbaric medicine.

MELVIN SHEFFIELD (1941–2018)

Melvin Sheffield

Melvin Sheffield, the eleventh child of Lyman and Litha Sheffield, was born on August 20, 1941 in Old Chicora (Polk County) near Brewster, Florida. He was two years old when his father died. Melvin attended Brewster Elementary School, Brewster Junior High School, and Mulberry High School in Polk County, Florida. In his teens, he was a member of the 4-H Club and Future Farmers of America (FFA) and showed beef animals at County and State Fairs. With the assistance of older brother, Carlos, in high school Melvin and Paul formed a Country and Western Band that entertained at high school assemblies. The band also entertained at the 1957 Florida State Fair in Tampa. Melvin played the mandolin and banjo, Paul played the guitar and harmonica, and two classmates played the fiddle and the washtub bass.

After high school, Melvin worked as a mechanic for 8 years at Florida Air Tool in Mulberry, Florida.

In 1965, Melvin married Sandra Faye Rentz who bore him three children, Leslie Melvin (1966), Elizabeth Faye (1967), and Robert Shawn (1971). That marriage did not last and in 1972 Melvin married Rebecca Jean Lamb and moved to Crossville, Tennessee where their three sons were born: Aaron Laverne (1973), James Truman (1974), and Jason Brooks (1982). In Crossville, Melvin had an automobile repair business where he was the mechanic and manager.

Rebecca Jean succumbed to cancer on September 8, 1989. During Melvin's lengthy illness with cancer, his treatments included radiation, chemotherapy and surgery. In 2000, he lost function of his left arm and was forced to close his automobile repair shop. Melvin died on February 24, 2018, at age 76. Melvin and Rebecca Jean's remains are at the Murray Memorial Gardens & Mausoleum in Murray, Kentucky.

AFTERWORD

This research began as a search for Susan's past in order to fill in names and dates on a genealogy chart. In addition to "Who Begat Whom," we found information to collect, record, and appreciate the people who have created this Sheffield Family Line.

REFERENCES

1. Joel W. Perry, Some Pioneer History of Early County, 1818-1871, p 45, 1968
2. Early County GA Deed Book page 12, Sept 20, 1887
3. Edgar Canter Brown, Florida's Peace River Frontier, University of Central Florida Press, 1991
4. Daniel H. Redfearn, Alexander McDonald of New Inverness Georgia and Descendants, Miami, FL, 1954.
5. Henry B. Guppy, Homes of Family Names in Great Britain, 1890. p15
6. Andrew Williams, A Sheffield Family History, 1995
7. War Soldiers' Graves, compiled by H. Ross Arnold, Jr. & H. Clifton Burnham. c1993 by the Georgia Society of the Sons of the American Revolution.
8. http://www.findagrave.com
9. Early County News, Blakeley Georgia, 1886-87.
10. Atlanta Constitution, Atlanta, Georgia, Oct 16, 1886.
11. US Census Records
12. LDS Genealogical Surveys
13. Tombstone inscriptions

APPENDIX LIST

Appendix A: Early Life in Old Chicora

Appendix B: Sheffield Lineage before Susan Delilah Sheffield

Appendix C: Newspaper Reports of Seaborn Sheffield's Murder in Early County News, Blakely, Georgia

Appendix D: Atlanta Constitution Newspaper Reports on Seaborn Sheffield's Murder, with editorial commentary on his life

Appendix E: Court Records of Those Charged with Seaborn Sheffield's Murder

Appendix F: The Civil War Days (1861-1865) and its impact on Freeman Sheffield's family

Appendix G: Other Stories of Events in the Author's Life

Story 1. The White Rose. Litha Sheffield's Death Notification

Story 2. The Three Block Journey

Story 3. The Disabled Christian

Story 4. Quick to Judge

Story 5. Value of Faith & Family

Story 6. The Homeless Lady

Story 7. The Lost Car

Story 8. Remembering My Brother Cob

APPENDIX A

EARLY LIFE IN OLD CHICORA

Excerpts from original publication in Polk County Historical Quarterly Vol 21, No 1, June 1994, p 4-5, with permission from the Polk County Historical Association on 21 Nov 2019.

EARLY LIFE IN OLD CHICORA

BY PAUL J. SHEFFIELD, PH.D.

I was born in 1940, the tenth of eleven children to Litha and Lyman Sheffield, who were share-crop farmers. They were blessed with a large family to help work the fields: Fern Lloyd, Edna Lois, Lesley, Ruby, Carlos, Letha, Edward, Cleveland, Tilmon, Paul James and Melvin. Two children (Lesley and Ruby) passed away in their youth. Dad lost his 7 -year bout with cancer in 1943, leaving Mom with 7 children still at home, ranging in age from 2 to 17. Soon thereafter, there would be four, as the older children dropped out of school to make their own way. It was a time of food and fuel rationing to support our servicemen in WWII, which was important to us since Lloyd was serving in the Pacific Theater. Lois and Letha married to raise their respective families; Carlos, or "Cob" would become a successful businessman; and Edward would become a most beloved preacher.

We were fortunate that, during the Great Depression, Dad had the foresight to purchase 20 acres of raw land in Old Chicora which consisted mostly of pines, palmetto and swamp. It was virgin land with rich topsoil that he would never have the opportunity to plow. Shortly after Dad's death in 1943, Mom and Carlos were able to sell enough pine trees to construct a house. Without benefit of carpenter's level or square, they built the modest, six-room house in which we would live and work the land. Our home lasted a half century surrounded by an orange grove. The only modifications had been a roof replacement, new boards in the porch floors, and indoor plumbing.

The 1940s in Old Chicora were difficult, but character-building, as the children took on adult roles early. Mom's frugality, determination, and loyalty to us, kept our family intact during those hard times. She threw nothing away. For many years, Dad's overalls hung on the closet door, serving as a daily reminder that we must make it without him. We wore hand-me-down overalls, provided by well-wishing neighbors. She made shirts from feed sacks and underwear from flour sacks. Scraps of cloth were sewn into quilts and worn-out stockings were woven into floor mats. We made soap from pork fat and lye and used it for the weekly laundry, which consisted of boiling the clothes in a washpot and hanging them on the clothesline to dry. Water was hand carried from a pitcher pump, which was eventually relocated from the field to the back porch. We had a "two-holer" outhouse made of discarded shingles from a neighbor's roof. Rainwater was diverted from the back porch roof into a large tank that was equipped with a nozzle and served as an outside shower. It didn't take much water to shower in the wintertime. Each person took responsibility for chores to help the family make it.

Grandpa John W. Cooley's catch in the creek on our land

We grew our own food. During summer and fall, we canned vegetables for the winter. In the winter, we slaughtered a hog, fried it in its own lard in an outside washpot, and stored the fried pork in 5-gallon cans of lard for use in the summer. Fried chicken was a Sunday treat. To supplement our food supply, we hunted rabbit and squirrel, caught gopher turtles, and fished in the prolific South Prong of the Alafia River, which crossed our land. We sometimes fished in Number 4 pool, which was about 4 miles away. Three milk cows provided milk and enough cream for butter, which we sold door-to-door in nearby Brewster. Sugar cane was squeezed and made into syrup, which we mixed with fresh butter to create a delicious dessert when sopped with biscuits or hoecake. The old wooden stove turned out some fine meals, despite the fact that the oven didn't heat evenly. Dinner was at noontime and supper was at night. We never considered ourselves poor, for "poor" was a state of mind, and we could always imagine someone who was worse off.

The REA installed electricity to the region when I was about twelve. Prior to that time, the only refrigeration was an icebox, for which ice was delivered once a week. We did our chores during the daylight and studied by kerosene lamp. A car radio was set up for listening to the Grand Ole Opry each Saturday night. Since most of our family could play a musical instrument, Sunday afternoon entertainment usually consisted of a country "hoedown." Emanating from the living room would be the old favorites: "Turkey in the Straw," "Alabama Jubilee," "San

Antonio Rose," "Kentucky Waltz" and "Orange Blossom Special."

We attended church every fourth and fifth Sunday at the old log Bethlehem Primitive Baptist Church. It was an all-day affair, with dinner on the grounds, making up for the Sundays that church was not conducted. Fourth Sunday was all-day preaching. Fifth Sunday was all-day *a cappella* singing. Periodic cemetery workings brought out the Chicora residents to hoe, rake and clean the grave sites, some of which were dated in the 1800s. In 1991, Mom joined Dad, their remains at rest in the cemetery she had worked so many times.

The 1950s brought easier times to Old Chicora. Mom got a job washing dishes at the Brewster School lunchroom. Carlos had a successful plumbing and electrical business in Fort Meade, where I worked during the summer and on weekends. We put in a 10-acre orange grove and planted the rest in Bahia grass for our cattle. Arrival of electricity ushered in a new environment of lights, running hot and cold water, indoor plumbing, refrigeration, electric stove, and a radio that we could listen to at any time. The county installed a concrete bridge across the Alafia River to replace the wooden one that had been repeatedly damaged and washed away by floods. They also paved Bethlehem Road, erasing forever the well-worn ruts originally created by the early settlers.

I attended Brewster Elementary and Junior High during 1946-54, completing the eighth grade in a class of eight students. During 1955-58, I attended Mulberry High School, graduated third in a class of 51 students, and was voted as the boy most likely to succeed. The salutatorian of my class, June Campbell, would later marry me.

I was active in 4-H and FFA, showing dairy and beef cattle at the various county and state fairs, and winning several public speaking contests. The Mulberry Kiwanis Club sponsored one of my steers. After Melvin and I left home in the late 1950s, Mom continued to live alone with her memories in the house she built. She proudly displayed our photos, ribbons and newspaper clippings in her living room.

But not all my 4-H projects were successful. My bee keeping project ended when swamp bees took up residence with the honey bees and dared me to collect the honey. I sold a registered Hereford cow to my neighbor for half her value one week before she calved, not knowing that the neighbor's bull had tip-toed over the fence. The fryers I raised were so tough that you couldn't drink the gravy from the smother-fried chicken.

Cleveland was working at the mines when a gasoline truck collided with his train and left him badly burned. Despite the limited use of his hands, he never lost his spirit or his strong work ethic. Seven years older than I, Tilmon would rather fight than eat, earning him the undisputed title of "Mean Tilmon." He was quite generous in his offer to "beat you and make you like it," but I don't recall ever having liked it. I was proud of his selection as May Day King at the Brewster May Day celebration, and missed him when he left home for a career in the Army. I am partly responsible for his current international notoriety, for many "Mean Tilmon" stories were sneaked into my lectures. One year younger than I, Melvin was my best friend in Old Chicora. A mechanical genius, he could tear up more things in one day than six skilled mechanics could fix in a week.

It was during a particularly hot day while Melvin and I were grubbing palmetto roots that I seriously questioned whether there might be an easier way to make a living, and college came to mind. Although I had received 2 small college scholarships through the Polk County Extension Service and the International Mining Corp, attendance seemed unlikely. It was the generosity of Kenneth and Mary Durrance, who invited me to reside with them, that made it possible for me to attend the University of Florida. Ken Durrance was on the faculty at the time, and would later become internationally known for his scientific advances in swine production. The Durrances provided the nurturing and encouragement that I needed for successful completion of a premed curriculum and a BS degree in Chemistry.

My Air Force career has limited the time available to visit family and friends in Old Chicora, but we have done so at each opportunity. Old Chicora produced some fine people: names like Albritton, Alderman, Benton, Colding, Dillard, Galbraith, Gant, Hutchinson, Jenkins, Lancaster, McNeal, Minton, Nicholson, Parker, Sheffield, Sherrod, Stanley, Taylor, and Twiss. The ones I knew were hard-working people of strong moral fiber, and they were outstanding Americans.

The "good old days" in Old Chicora were character building indeed. Although times were hard, we were much better off than people in similar situations today. We could depend on the land and the waterways for survival.

There were many lessons learned from my early experience in Old Chicora. First, a single-parent family can make it in hard times, but it is very difficult. In our case, the children had to drop out of school and become adults far earlier than they should. Second, many doors of opportunity are open to young people, making anything achievable. But every life decision they make closes some of the doors and limits their future to those that remain open. Choosing the path of education seems to keep the maximum number of doors open. Regrettably, only three of my siblings were able to complete high school, one of whom graduated after age 40. Third, having the determination to do well is a good start, but it is unlikely to happen unless surrounding folks care enough to encourage and help the person along the way. Fortunately for me, I was chosen by several people who wanted to help me. Fourth, hard work pays off. It seems that the harder I worked, the luckier I got. Finally, tools for success came from many sources: Chicora's tough environment; a supportive family; the "day's work for a day's pay" work ethic; and practical knowledge derived from teachers, such as Ms. Avery, Mr. Choate, Ms. Clarke, Mr. Dudek, Ms. Frazier, Mr. Pugh, Mr. Ross and Ms. Weaver. These wonderful people saw through the coarse exterior of this backward farm boy and made him feel like he was capable of doing something special!

ABOUT THE AUTHOR BY RAY ALBRITTON

Doctor Paul J. Sheffield is a former resident of Old Chicora, an old community in the Southwest corner of Polk County. He attended Brewster Elementary and Junior High School (1946- 54), Mulberry High School (1954-58). He received a BS in Chemistry from the University of Florida (1962), and a MS and PhD in Physiology from the University of Southern California (1971, 72). In 1962, he joined the US Air Force. He became an Aerospace Physiologist to teach aircrew the medical aspects of high-altitude flight. He helped create the first Air Force clinical hyperbaric medicine center and his research helped scientifically show the benefits of this treatment method for modern medicine.

Promotions to increasingly responsible jobs eventually led to the top job for an Aerospace Physiologist in the Office of the Air Force Surgeon General at Washington, DC. In September 1992, he retired in the grade of Colonel, after 30 years of service.

Dr. Sheffield is a past president of two international professional societies: Aerospace Physiology Society, and Undersea and Hyperbaric Medical Society. He is a member of the Phi Kappa Phi Honor Society. Dr. Sheffield and his wife, June have two sons James and Robert. Dr. Sheffield is one of the 1994 inductees in the Polk County Schools' Hall of Fame.

APPENDIX B

SHEFFIELD LINEAGE BEFORE
SUSAN DELILAH SHEFFIELD

In 1995, Andrew M. Williams published *A Sheffield Family History* that traces the family lineage from Thomas Sheffield (1550-1598) of England. A synopsis of his report is included herein for completeness of record. Our research has confirmed the lineage beginning with William Sheffield (1700-1764), but we did not attempt to confirm the Sheffield lineage prior to 1700.

- Elisham Sheffield (1530-1549) b. England, d. England; m. Mary Allison
- Thomas Sheffield (1550-1598) b. England, d. Sudbury, England; m. Myra
- Edmund Sheffield (1580-1630) b. England, d. Ballingdon, England; m. Thomazize
- Ichabod Sheffield (1630-1712) b. Sudbury, England, d. Newport RI, USA m. Mary Parker
- Ichabod Sheffield (1669- 1736) b. South Kingston RI, m. Elizabeth Manchester

- William Sheffield (1700-1764) b. South Kingston RI, m. Mary B. Abbott
- John Sheffield (1728-1790) b. Virginia, d. Duplin County, NC, m. (1) Elizabeth West, (2) Elizabeth Graddy
- Bryan Sheffield (1781-1847) b. 1781, Duplin County, NC, d. 1847 Early County, GA, m. Nancy Paine
- Seaborn Sheffield (1821-1886) b. Early County GA, d. Early County GA
- Sarah Sheffield (1825-?) b. Early County GA, m. Reuben McCorquodale
- Russia Sheffield (1829-1891) b. Early County GA, m. William Sasser
- Prussia Sheffield (1831-1922) b. Early County GA m. John Aubrey Timmons
- Delilah Bryant Sheffield (1835-1900) b. Early County GA, m. George W. Mayes
- Freeman Sheffield (1832-1881) b. Early County GA, m. Celia Brown
    (1) Elizabeth Sheffield (1856)
    (2) Susan Delilah Sheffield (1857)
    (3) Freeman Sheffield (1859)
    (4) Samuel J. Sheffield (1861)
    (5) John W. Sheffield (1863)
    (6) Mary Sheffield (1866)

NEWSPAPER REPORTS OF SEABORN SHEFFIELD'S MURDER IN EARLY COUNTY NEWS, BLAKELY, GEORGIA

"Homicide in Early County. On Friday night last, about bedtime, someone, as yet unknown, stealthily approached the door, or window, of Mr. Seaborn Sheffield's house, while Mr. S. was quietly sitting at his table, where he had been writing, and shot him in the back of the head, killing him instantly. A Negro man, who usually slept in the room with Mr. Sheffield, was lying in the doorway asleep, but was awakened by the discharge of the gun, and at once went to some of the cabins nearby and reported the killing. Soon a considerable crowd had assembled, and a messenger was sent to Blakely for the Coroner, who went on Saturday morning to hold an inquest over the body. No evidence was developed as to who did the killing, but an anonymous letter was found on the person or premises of the deceased, which threatened his life. The letter had been dropped in the post office at Arlington on the previous afternoon, as was stated by the

Postmaster. It is said to have been written in a good hand, but with an attempt at disguise. The deceased was quite infirm, and was over sixty years old. He had recently made a will, which had given dissatisfaction to some parties, and it is supposed by some that the dissatisfied parties took this foul way of revenging themselves. Whoever did it seemed not to remember the old adage, 'Murder will out,' and are probably now resting in a fancied security that will fail them when they least expect it. No effort should be spared to ferret out the villainous murderer or murderers, whoever they be. Our Grand Jury meets next week, and it is to be hoped they will use all vigilance in endeavoring to bring to light the perpetrators of the crime." [Early County News, Vol XXVII (16), Thurs, Sept 30, 1886, p 3.]

"Six hundred head of cattle belonging to the estate of Seaborn Sheffield, who was killed near Arlington last Friday night will be sold on the 9th of October at public outcry." [Early County News, Vol XXVII (16), Thurs, Sept 30, 1886.]

"Governor McDaniel has offered a reward of $150 for the arrest of the unknown murderers of Mr. Seaborn Sheffield, with proof to convict. His proclamation may be found in another column." [Early County News, Blakely GA, Vol. XXVII (17), Oct 7, 1886]

ATLANTA CONSTITUTION NEWSPAPER REPORT ON SEABORN SHEFFIELD'S MURDER WITH EDITORIAL COMMENTARY ON HIS LIFE

The following article appeared on the front page of the Atlanta Constitution, Atlanta, Georgia, October 15, 1886. It provides the newspaper reporter's view of Seaborn Sheffield's life, the threat by the KKK on his life, and put forth the theories of citizens regarding the murder. The Atlanta Constitution article was not only unkind to Seaborn, but it was also inaccurate, showing him as the only son of Bryan (ignoring Freeman), stating that he had three daughters instead of two, and overestimating his land holdings as it described his murder. At the time of his death, Seaborn's estate had declined in value to about $9,000.

SHEFFIELD'S SINS: THE END OF A DESPICABLE CAREER

The Story of an Assassination—The Live of the Murdered Man—His Loves and Peccadilloes

—A Mixed Family of White and Black—the Ku Klux Notice--Etc, Etc

ARLINGTON, Ga., October 15 – (Special) – While Seaborn Sheffield, one of the wealthiest citizens of southwest Georgia, was sitting at his table counting his money, the loud report of a shotgun was heard, followed by still another. It was at a late hour in the evening. Tom Maury, a colored boy, who was asleep in the room, was awakened by the shots, when a horrible night presented itself to his eyes. There, by the table upon which was sitting a flickering lamp, sat the aged man, his head dropped upon the table, and his blood flowing in pools over the bank bills which he was in the act of counting. The bullets had shattered the lamp shade and passed through the head and shoulders of the dying man. While the affrighted negro was taking in the situation, he heard the sound of retreating hoofs and by the time he reached the door riders were too far gone to distinguish them. In a few minutes Ben Taliaferro and Rufus Lawrence, the sons-in-law of the murdered man, together with their wives, were on the spot. The alarm was spread rapidly through the county, but there seemed to be but little desire to hunt down the assassins.

MR SHEFEILD'S LIFE

Mr. Shefeild (spelled as in the printed article) was the son of one of the original pioneers of this county, having been raised in boyhood among the Indians. His father was a notable man, and accumulated quite a fortune. His children were Seaborn and three sisters. The sisters married men who have become prominent and well to do, rearing large families. Seaborn, however, lived a bachelor all his life, thoroughly irreligious, and only enjoying his passions and accumulating lands and cattle. He had at the time of his death 15,000 acres of the best land in the county; 1,000 head of cattle, besides other important interests, which made him a very rich man for this section of the country.

AMOURS IN WHITE AND BLACK

This man's amours in white and black have been the scandal of the community for forty years. He lived alone in a rather shabby house, where he carried on a life which would shame a Turk. In his younger days he confined himself principally to white conquests, the illicit results of which were three daughters. These girls he finally took to his home, and for a time it looked as if the parental instinct would save him. He appeared to love the children, took great pleasure in their company, and finally, when they grew large enough, he sent them for several terms to a female college, where they became quite accomplished and returned home charming young ladies. It was then that they were shocked by the discovery that their father had installed in the house, as their brother, a mulatto named John Sheffield. The old man insisted upon keeping his variegated family under the same roof, while he still continued his disgraceful career with the abandoned women of the neighborhood. Quarrels ensued in which the father invariably clung to the cause of his black son. The girls finally married respectable young farmers, and leaving home, John Sheffield became the exclusive idol of his father's heart.

PREFERRING BLACK TO WHITE

Sheffield, on taking his daughters to his home, had formally adopted them as his own. He opposed their marriages violently, and never became reconciled to his sons-in-law, while they, in turn, had but little respect for the shameless Mormon. John Sheffield, holding such a warm place in his father's affections, gained a certain amount of respect from those who honored the old man's gold. He openly married a white woman, though it was a violation of the law which prohibits the union of whites and blacks. This marriage met with his father's full approval, and ever after, the old man was on the warmest terms with his mulatto son and grandchildren.

It was then that John, seeing the complete mastery he had over his father, became carried away with his importance, and fell under the displeasure of the whole community. Frequent raids would be made on Mr Sheffield's herds by cattle thieves. John would lay the blame first on one neighbor and then on another. Many of them were thus arrested and taken to court, only to be acquitted after much loss of time and the payment of lawyer's fees. These continual raids, and consequent arrests of innocent parties, aroused the people to the necessity of self-protection. A vigilance committee was formed, which had but little difficulty in discovering that John himself was the thief, stealing the cattle and selling them in the Albany market. As soon as he discovered that the people were on his trail, John skipped out, and found refuge in Alabama. Seaborn Sheffield grew furious over what he regarded as slanders upon his son's fair name. He scoured the country to find the thief, finally bringing him back to the paternal roof. He did not do this, however, until he had spent about $5,000 disposing of the charges against his son.

THE RIVALRY FOR THE PROPERTY

Seaborn Sheffield had reached his sixty-fifth year, and was very feeble. He claimed that the persecution of his son John, as he called it, was instigated by his daughters, who wished to get him out of the way, so that they might get all his property. During the first week in September he was heard to declare that he would will his property to his negro son, and cut off his white daughters altogether.

On the day before the assassination Mr. Sheffield received, through the post office, the following letter, which was found on his dead body:

Headquarters K.K.K – You, Seaborn Sheffield, are hereby notified that your case has been duly considered, and the fact that you have, or inted (sp) giving your property to John Sheffield, duly considered, and now, unless you make a good and lawful will in the next thirty days, giving your entire property to your white daughters, it has been fully decided that, between two suns, you shall be riddled with buckshot and your degraded soul sent to the hell where it belongs. "A hint, etc."

By order of the captain Bloody Bones.

Raw Head, Secretary and First Serg't.

This was written on the envelope.

"If not delivered in ten days, return to Raw Head and Bloody Bones."

The letter was written in a plain, legible, business handwriting, was punctuated as above and the writer apparently attempted to disguise his chirography by writing backhand.

THE THEORIES ADVANCED

In the excitement consequent upon the announcement of the assassination, rumors were rife as to who could have been the guilty party. Some thought the assassins were some of the men who had been so ruthlessly prosecuted in connection with the cattle stealing, while others believe that John Sheffield, in the belief that his father had already made the will in his favor, committed the crime in order to gain speedy possession of the property. The most singular theory of all, however, comes from the dead man's three sisters. Knowing that their brothers' children, white as well as black, were equally illegitimate, the aunts naturally antagonize them all, and believe that the property should revert back to the blood kin in lawful wedlock. Consequently, these old ladies say that Mr. Rufus Lawrence, Mr. Sheffield's son-in-law, committed the deed, and they adduce as their reason for alleging it, that every time Mr. Lawrence approached the dead body during the night, the wound gaped and bled afresh. They affirm that this is positive and convicting evidence.

Investigation, however, fails to clinch the crime upon anyone, and the only satisfactory feature of the whole tragedy is the discovery that Mr. Sheffield had made no will, and that in consequence of his having lawfully adopted his white daughters, they will come into possession of the estate. [Atlanta Constitution, October 15, 1886, p 1.]

APPENDIX E

COURT RECORDS OF THOSE CHARGED WITH SEABORN SHEFFIELD'S MURDER

Seaborn Sheffield was murdered on September 24, 1886. Local authorities thought that the most likely suspects were his sons-in-law Rufus Lawrence and Ben Taliaferro so they were charged with the crime. After dragging on for 18 months, the case was eventually dismissed.

Apr T (term) 1887 #222. The State vs Rufus Lawrence and Ben Taliaferro; Charge: Murder; Lawyers: HC Sheffield, WD Kiddoo, C Wilson. In jail. Taliaferro-bailed in $1000/ Lawrence's bail fixed by consent of Solicitor at $1500/ & the case cont'd Oct T 87. Contd by the State for want of witnesses. Set for 8 AM of Tuesday, 2nd week, of next term/ Apr T 88. Nol. Pros. allowed at request of Sol & prosecuting parties on assurances that there is not evidence to justify trial [Criminal Docket 1883-188_, Early County Superior Court, p 45.]

"Messrs. Rufus Lawrence and Ben Taliaferro were recently arrested and lodged in the Blakely jail under indictment for the murder of their father-in-law, Seaborn Sheffield, the former as principal and the latter as accessory. We know nothing about the circumstances or the evidence under which they were indicted and are not prepared to express an opinion as to the guilt or innocence of the prisoners. The charge is a serious one and should be fully and carefully investigated. Being unable to come to trial at this term of Court, the Judge granted bail to Taliaferro yesterday before adjournment of court, in the sum of $1,000 at the request of counsel and the consent of the Solicitor General. The application of Lawrence for bail will be heard in the near future and the question of granting his application considered on the merits of evidence against him." [Early County News, Blakely Georgia, Vol XXVII (44), Thurs 14 Apr 1887.]

"Early Superior Court. Court adjourned on Friday morning of last week and reassembled on Monday morning of this week. The case of the State vs. Rufus Lawrence and Ben Taliaferro, charged with the murder of Seaborn Sheffield was called, but the Solicitor announced that the State was not ready, and the case was postponed until April term, 1888, Tuesday morning of the second week, at eight o'clock." [Early County News, Blakely Georgia, Oct 13, 1887.]

"The State vs Rufus Lawrence, Ben Taliaferro: Murder. It being shown to the court that the person prosecuting this case ask that it be Nol Prossed and also that a conviction could not now be asked or expected under the evidence as it now exists. This known and the Defendants being in court and ready for bail at the request of the Solicitor General, it is ordered that the Solicitor have leave to enter a Solle prosequi on this Bill, April 10, 1888. John T Clarke, JSCPC. And now comes JH Guerry, Sol Gen and enters a Solle Prosequi on this Bill, April 10th 1888. JH Guerry, Sol Gen." [Minutes of Early Superior Court, 1887-1982, Apr 10, 1888, p 116.]

"Superior Court...Rufus Lawrence and Ben Taliaferro, charged with the murder of Seaborn Sheffield. Case nolle prossed." (The case was dismissed.) [Early County News, Blakely Georgia, Apr 12, 1888.]

APPENDIX F

THE CIVIL WAR DAYS (1861-1865) AND ITS IMPACT ON FREEMAN SHEFFIELD'S FAMILY

With freedom of the slaves as an issue, the Civil War between the North (the Union) and the South (the Confederacy) occurred during 1861 to 1865. Like farmers in most of the southern states, many of the Early County plantation owners held slaves to work the crops. The Emancipation Proclamation issued by President Abraham Lincoln, effective January 1, 1863, freed all slaves in all territories still at war with the Union. Some of the freed people moved away in search of a better life. Others remained on the land as employees or sharecroppers, some of whom took the family name of their former masters. According to Early County and Miller County census records, it was common for Sheffield landowners to have farm laborers or domestic servants remaining with them that were recorded as Sheffield. There is no record of anyone remaining on Freeman's farm, so his children became the primary farm laborers.

Fearing an uprising from the 5092 slaves in the county, the Early County Inferior Court directed a list of men 55-60 years of age to act as police in the county:

> "In compliance with a recent order of the Commander-in-Chief authorizing the exemption of 1 man for every 500 Negroes, we have made the following exemptions for this county."

BW Sheffield and Arthur Sheffield (Bryant's brother) were on the list, but it was noted that Arthur was unable to perform police duty [Minutes of the Early County Superior Court, August 6, 1863].

No record was found of Freeman's participation in the Civil War. Like other farmers in the area, it is likely that his role was to produce food for the soldiers and their families. BW Sheffield was instructed by Early Inferior Court to serve as agent to collect corn and distribute to families of the soldiers:

> "...receive tithe corn from all planters in his vicinity giving duplicate receipts for the same and distribute the same to such soldiers families and other very indigent persons, and in such quantities as he may in his judgement deem best for the interest of said families." [Minutes of the Early County Superior Court, April 19, 1865].

Salt, crucial for curing meat, was in low supply. Early County wives of soldiers in service were entitled to 1/2 bushel of salt for $1, and widows of deceased soldiers were entitled to 1/2 bushel of salt without charge, under Georgia Governor Joseph E. Brown's order to the Commissary General [Minutes of the Early County Superior Court, July 31, 1862]. On August 6 1863, Governor Brown directed further distribution of salt to soldiers' families and directed the County Treasurer to remit $4 to each family from the County Military Fund. [Minutes of the Early County Superior Court, August 6, 1863].

By September 1864, there were 317 families depending on the County Military Fund: 175 wives, 64 widows of deceased soldiers, 47 widows with sons in service, 9 families depending on soldiers, and 19 disabled discharged soldiers. [Minutes of the Early County Superior Court, September 26, 1864]. No person named Sheffield was on the list.

Shortage of food and hard times was illustrated by Aunt Linnie Sheffield Fowler's story of Grandmother Susan preparing three hoecakes each morning. "For breakfast they would eat one hoecake. She would wrap one in her apron to take to the fields for dinner (noon meal). Upon returning home in the evening, they would eat the third hoecake for supper. The traditional hoecake was made of cornmeal and was cooked on a flat cast iron bread pan called a hoe. Hoecake was also referred to as ashcake and pone. A close relative, corn pone, was also made of corn meal. [Linnie Sheffield Fowler. A personal communication, 1996]

In the 1940s, when I was a preschooler in Old Chicora, Florida, stories of the Civil War were still being told by older relatives. They gave me nightmares! Grandpa John Cooley told a story about a Confederate Army deserter who, when found by Confederate soldiers, was stripped of his clothing, covered with molasses, feathered, and carried through the streets on a rail. He would give great detail about how the soldiers searched the property and found the molasses hidden in the barn and they got feathers by ripping open a mattress. Aunt Linnie told a story about a Confederate Army deserter who hid so effectively that he could not be found. Confederate soldiers found his small daughter and killed her when she would not tell where her father was hiding. The child's grave was near the local store that Aunt Linnie frequently passed as a young girl. Hardy family genealogy records show that William Aaron Hardy's grandfather was in the Civil War and was said to have been a deserter from the Confederate Army. Aunt Linnie had also heard that story from her Grandpa Hardy. [Linnie Sheffield Fowler. A personal communication, 1996]

APPENDIX G

OTHER STORIES OF EVENTS IN THE AUTHOR'S LIFE

These stories were sent by the author to Reverend Donald Chandler, Associational Missionary/Director of Missions for the Eastern Panhandle of West Virginia for use in his sermons.

STORY 1: THE WHITE ROSE

On 22 June 1991, the excitement waned on my final day as President of the Undersea and Hyperbaric Medical Society (UHMS). I received telephone notification of my Mother's death about 15 minutes before I was to give the President's Address at the 1991 UHMS Annual Awards Banquet in San Diego, California. It was a time of deep sorrow! However, from Mom I had learned on the farm that no matter how gloomy the day, the crops must be harvested. So, I put on my fake happy face and presided over the gala event.

As I struggled with my composure to give the speech, the recurrent thought going through my mind was "Where is my white rose?" Roses have always had a special place in my heart. My Mom always wore a white rose on Mother's Day to identify that her Mother was deceased, and I wore a red rose to show my Mother was alive. She also used roses to teach us lessons of life. When I was young, Mom took me to the cowshed, gave me a rose, and asked me to scatter the petals. Then she pointed and asked, "What is that?" I responded that it was a cow pie with rose petals on it. She said, "That's right, son. No matter how many rose petals you scatter over it, a cow pie is still a cow pie."

It had been 21 years since Mom's death when one of my friends in the UHMS was getting grief from her narcissistic boss, so I told her my Mom's cow pie story. Her response was "I will always look at a rose petal differently now." I also told her about my struggle at the UHMS meeting when Mom passed away: "Where's my white rose?" The following morning, I had a moving experience when a lovely arrangement of a dozen white roses arrived from San Diego, the site of the 1991 UHMS Annual Scientific Meeting. I did not realize that my friend's response would mean so much to me after such a long time. It seems that it is never too late to need an act of kindness.

STORY 2: THE THREE BLOCK JOURNEY

Within 15 minutes I was to be on stage to give the final presentation in the course. Sixty doctors and nurses from 20 states were waiting to graduate and depart for home to celebrate the Christmas Holiday. From my office, the classroom was a ten-minute walk, so I had plenty of time to make it.

As I walked through the hospital lobby, my attention was drawn to a middle-aged patient sitting in a wheelchair and thanking the receptionist for the loan of it. He had a cane and was having so much difficulty trying to stand that I offered to help him. He explained that he had come to see the surgeon because of trouble walking and the surgeon had told him that both his knees had to be replaced. I asked him to sit in the wheelchair and I would push him out to the sidewalk so he could get a cab. Once outside, he explained that before going home he needed to go to the pharmacy for some pain medicine. The pharmacy was only three blocks away and was on the way to the classroom. But I would have to bring the wheelchair back to the hospital and that would make me late. The cell phone rang with a message the students were waiting. I apologized for not being able to take him to the pharmacy. He said, "That's OK. I can make it." He knew that a three-block walk would be virtually impossible for him, but he was determined to make it.

I helped him out of the wheelchair but it was so difficult that I asked him to return to the wheelchair so I could push him to the pharmacy. He said, "But the doctors and nurses are waiting on you." I reassured him that the doctors and nurses would understand. Sometimes a person needs a little help along the way.

We slowly made our way to the pharmacy. The sidewalk was filled with holiday shoppers and sightseers that we had to navigate around. We had to cross two busy streets that were filled with holiday traffic. We finally arrived at the pharmacy where he thanked me, and we parted.

I had walked that path to and from my office well over a hundred times. Yet I had never seen the difficulty that this short 3-block journey would cause a person who had trouble walking. The pathway was wheelchair friendly, but not friendly for a lame person. Hazards were everywhere to cause trips, slips, and falls. There were uneven areas in the sidewalk to trip him. In the absence of handrails, the sloped areas for wheelchairs were too steep for him to walk without slipping. He could not step off the curb to cross the street without the risk of falling. His pace was so slow that he could not walk across the street before the light changed. I had not previously seen these things because I had not walked in his shoes.

As I rushed to the classroom, I was reminded of the 1960s song by Joe South and the Believers "Walk a Mile in My Shoes."

If I could be you, if you could be me for just one hour
If we could find a way to get inside each other's mind,
If you could see you through my eyes instead of your ego
I believe you'd be surprised to see that you've been blind.
Walk a mile in my shoes, walk a mile in my shoes
Hey, before you abuse, criticize and accuse
Walk a mile in my shoes

On hearing the explanation for my tardiness, the doctors and nurses understood. Every day they see people struggle with health problems. They understood the need for perspective and compassion. They understood that often all the person needs is a little help along the way.

STORY 3: THE DISABLED CHRISTIAN

As I was in route to my office Sunday afternoon, an elderly man was stranded in the island between 4 lanes of traffic. The traffic was sparse as I neared his location, so I stopped in the street and ask if he needed help. He told me that he was headed to the Cathedral to praise God for his blessings, but he was having trouble making it. He had pushed his walker to this location and could walk no longer in the intense heat, so he had sat on his walker seat and shuffled his feet trying to make it move up the inclining street. He was simply too frail and lacked the strength to make it up the incline. I pushed him in his walker across the street, helped him into the car, and we drove about a mile to the Cathedral. Once there, the wheelchair access was an incline made of cobble stone creating yet another hurdle for him. We finally arrived at the Cathedral entrance where other worshipers greeted him.

This aging Christian had made this journey previously so he knew it would be difficult. He did not know what was in store for him today, but he had set out determined to make it to the Cathedral so he could praise his Savior. All he needed to make it was a little help along the way.

We are all very proud of our achievements, but it is doubtful that any of us achieve anything of value without having a little help along the way.

STORY 4: QUICK TO JUDGE

Friday morning, I gave a presentation at a local hotel and was walking to the hospital when I saw a young man in a motorized wheelchair having difficulty crossing the street. I asked him if I could help. He removed a cigarette from his mouth and explained several features of the wheelchair that made it difficult for him to operate. As we crossed the street, he told me of his medical condition that had confined him to the wheelchair. When we got to the other side of the street, we saw a crumpled dollar bill that someone had left on the sidewalk. He remarked "The

Lord works in mysterious ways. I really need that dollar." He put the cigarette in his mouth to free his gnarled fingers so he could pick up the dollar and put it in his shirt pocket. My immediate thought was, "Yes, you need the dollar, but you need the cigarette more."

Saturday morning, I saw him again at the same street corner, but he had no cigarette. While I waited for the light to change, he waved and called, "Hello, my friend!" A woman, who appeared to be a resident of the streets, approached him in her wheelchair. As she neared, they touched fingertips. Then he took the crumpled dollar bill from his shirt pocket and gave it to her. It was then I realized I had judged him too quickly.

Saturday afternoon I came across him at a different street corner near the hospital. There was a sense of urgency in his voice as he asked if I could help him. He said that a restaurant had just given him food, but he needed ten dollars for bus fare. Having witnessed his act of kindness earlier in the day, I gave him the ten dollars. He wept as he thanked me. Shortly thereafter, from the hospital lobby I could see him wheeling his chair in the direction of the bus station.

From a safe position on the shore, it is easy to tell a drowning man how to swim. But sometimes he also needs a little help along the way. Unlike this fellow, I don't think I would have the courage to give my last dollar to a needy person and then beg for a ride or something to eat.

STORY 5: VALUE OF FAITH AND FAMILY

When I was young, the Sunday comics were a primary source of entertainment. Al Capp's Li'l Abner comic strip was a favorite. Among the characters was Joe Btfsplk, the world's worst jinx. He was a little guy with the wide brim hat and the ever-present black cloud floating over his head. Whenever Joe showed up in Al Capp's comic strip, a disaster happened. Of course, we youngsters knew that no such person existed.

Now 65 years later, I met a man named Jeremy whose string of bad luck reminds me of Joe Btfsplk. Here is a summary of a thirteen-day encounter with Jeremy. It is a story of a man down on his luck trying to raise money to rejoin his family and visit a dying father. Throughout it all, Jeremy never stopped trying and never lost his faith.

Day 1: I was walking to my mailbox in the hot Texas sun when a man got out of a 1972 Chevrolet truck parked in the neighbor's yard and walked quickly toward me carrying a cat in his arms. He introduced himself as Jeremy and told me how much joy the cat brought to his life. He started listing his troubles and explained how he needed work to earn enough money to join his family in Alabama. He also wanted to see his father who was near death in the hospital. He had come to Texas to be with friends and start a tree trimming service. The business had not worked out and he had lost his home, so his wife took the kids and drove to Alabama to be with family. He quoted me a price to trim the oak trees on my property and to make minor repairs to the roof. After a brief discussion, we decided to start the project at 10:00 am each day so the noise would not disturb the neighbors. It was estimated to be a three-day job.

Day 2: Instead of 10:00 am, Jeremy, David and the cat arrived at about 3:00 pm. The side of the truck had been crushed by another vehicle. The truck had a fuel line problem that had taken all morning to fix. The cat took possession of the front yard. A resident deer saw the cat as a threat to her new fawn, stamped the ground a couple of times, then charged the cat. He narrowly escaped and spent the rest of the day hiding under the truck. They trimmed trees until dark.

Day 3: Jeremy, David, and the cat arrived at about 6:00 pm. When he replaced the fuel line, Jeremy had damaged the carburetor which then had to be special ordered because of the age of the truck. They trimmed trees until dark.

Day 4: Jeremy and the cat arrived at about 4:00 pm. Jeremy had a large cut above his right eye. Earlier in the morning, David (the guy who was supposed to climb up on my roof to repair it) had an epileptic seizure while they were driving to the job. Jeremy was able to fend off most of the flailing until he could stop the truck beside the road and wait until the seizure ended. He had then taken David to the hospital and waited with him until David's family arrived. Jeremy sobbed as he told me of his own father being in the hospital with no visitors and his father's long battle with chronic alcoholism that had destroyed his liver. He talked about his faith and credited his faith for being able to endure all these hardships. Since his cell phone had been stolen, he used my phone to call his wife and mother. He told them how much he loved them and how he was trying to finish the job and get the truck repaired so he could drive it to Alabama to join them.

Day 5: About 11:00 am Jeremy called from a service station to ask that I pick him up where his truck had broken down on the previous evening. He and the cat had spent the night in the truck which was parked behind the service station adjacent to some homeless men whose pit bull had harassed the cat. I met him and we went to the auto parts store to get more parts to repair the truck.

Day 6: About 2:00 pm Jeremy arrived with the cat and a new helper named Richard. He introduced Richard as a former employee whom Jeremy had previously fired because of his drinking on the job, but he was now sober. They arrived towing a borrowed trailer with a flat tire that had blown out while enroute to the job. Jeremy borrowed my tree saw and leaf blower—and broke both of them. After loading the tree trimmings on the trailer, the wheel was removed and placed in the flatbed of Jeremy's truck so he could find a replacement tire. The loaded trailer was left in the yard with a missing wheel.

Day 9: About 3:00 pm Jeremy called from a store to ask if I could pick him up at his truck which had stalled about 2 miles from my house. Jeremy, Richard and the cat had arrived at the job two hours earlier to replace the tire but discovered that the new tire is not on the truck. They retraced their route and discovered that the tire had fallen off the truck during a turn and was in the ditch along with his sleeping bag. Shortly after recovering the tire, the truck had stalled. We loaded the tire in my vehicle and took it to install on the trailer. Jeremy requested that we use my vehicle to take the loaded trailer back to its owner. I then declared the project finished and paid the bill. When we returned to Jeremy's truck, it started up so he drove it to a nearby restaurant that had given him permission to park it. He told me that he and the cat had been living in the truck for the past 4 days. Richard offered Jeremy a room for the night, so I drove them all downtown.

Day 11: Jeremy's mother and wife called separately to ask if I knew his whereabouts. I did not know because I had dropped him, Richard, and the cat off at a service station near Richard's apartment. I didn't know Richard's last name or his apartment address. I could only tell them where Jeremy's truck was located.

Day 13: About 4:00 pm a car entered my driveway driven by Jeremy's wife. She had returned to Texas to take him back to Alabama to attend his father's funeral. Jeremy asked if I could loan him some gas money to make the trip. He said Richard had set him up to be robbed by asking him to go to a nearby store and, as he exited the apartment, he was robbed at gunpoint. No longer able to trust Richard, he and the cat had been living in his truck, which enabled his wife to find him. The truck was inoperable, and all of his equipment had now been stolen except for four tools that he had left at my house.

Day 14: About 6:00 pm I received an emotional call from Jeremy thanking me. They had made the trip safely from Texas and were pulling into his mother's driveway in Alabama.

I have pondered over this story. How can someone deal with such a constant barrage of disappointments? It seems that Jeremy got the strength to endure from his faith and love of family. All he needed was a little help along the way.

STORY 6: THE HOMELESS LADY

I left the office and walked to the street intersection. Stranded in the street was a middle-aged lady in a wheelchair. She was wailing and sobbing as she struggled to get the wheelchair out of the street. Her left leg was amputated at the knee and her left arm had an open wound from the elbow to the wrist that was badly inflamed. Her right arm and leg were not sufficient to get the wheelchair up over the 1-inch ledge to move it up onto the sidewalk. Four people were standing there watching her struggle and cry.

As I approached, I asked if I could help her. She sobbed, "Just kill me. I have nothing to live for." As I pushed her onto the sidewalk, she continued: "I was on heroin, so they took my two kids away. Even though I am off drugs, my husband kicked me out of the house, so I have been living on the streets in this wheelchair for two weeks. Last night they robbed me. I asked a policeman for help but he couldn't help me. This morning I fell out of my wheelchair in the middle of the street and couldn't get up. Cars drove around me, but nobody would stop to help me back onto my wheelchair. Why won't they help me? Just kill me. I have nothing to live for."

I asked about her injuries. She explained that she had been hit by a bus that crushed her leg and burned her arm. I offered to take her to the hospital to treat her wounds, but she didn't want to go because she couldn't afford the doctor bill, explaining that her husband had emptied her bank account before kicking her out of the house. She accepted my offer to go get medication and bandages for her and she agreed to wait for me on the street.

A man walked by smoking a cigarette. She called to him, so he took a cigarette out of the pack and handed it to her. She reached into her pocket and gave him two quarters. She explained that she needed a cigarette to calm down.

As I returned with the medical supplies, I was astonished by how efficiently she was able to use the supplies and wrap her arm using only one hand and her teeth. She thanked me for the medical supplies and said she felt much better.

We talked about her going to a shelter to get off the street. I called my assistant who contacted 3 shelters in the city. None could accept her because they were all filled to capacity.

Haven for Hope was willing to allow her to sleep in their courtyard. Haven for Hope is a huge $100 million homeless center built by the city of San Antonio in 2007. According to San Antonio Express News reports, at any given time, about 850 people live on the Haven of Hope campus as they work to transition from homelessness. An additional 700 come and go to the outdoor courtyard each day, getting free food and access to showers and toilets, but they are not part of the transformation program. Of those, about 600 sleep there each night. This lady explained that people going to Haven for Hope have drugs with them, and she wanted to avoid the temptation.

She asked me to call her husband saying "He is a good man. He would not want me sleeping on the streets." I called the number she gave me and got a message that nobody was home. She took the phone, and while she was leaving a message, her husband answered. There was a brief discussion about where he could meet her. Then suddenly she yelled at him and hung up. I asked why she yelled at him while asking him for help. She responded: "He called me a druggie and I am no longer a druggie." She then announced that she was going to wait for her husband at the location they discussed. If he did not show up, she would be going to Haven for Hope that evening. Each day I pass that intersection I wonder what happened to her.

I am reminded of the poem about four candles: Peace, Faith, Love and Hope. When the candles of Peace, Faith, and Love burned out, the candle of Hope was used to relight them. Even though she was down and out, she had pride. In order to recover, she also needed hope; and she needed a little help along the way.

STORY 7: THE LOST CAR

As I entered the elevator to leave the hospital, an elderly gentleman in the elevator beside me said: "I don't know where I parked my car. I have seen three doctors at 3 different hospitals today and I don't know where I parked it." He explained that his memory was getting bad and that his family was insisting on his moving into an assisted living facility, but he was refusing to do it.

I was reminded of the birthday card I saw with the inscription on the front: *"Can hardly feel my hands and feet anymore. Can't remember if I'm 69 or 96. Have lost all my friends."* Inside the card was the message: *"But, thank God I still have my driver's license."*

I told the gentleman that I would help him find his car. We walked through the parking areas on 3 floors of our hospital without finding his car. We then drove my car through the parking lots at 2 nearby hospitals without finding it. As we were returning to our hospital he pointed to a car on the street: "That's my car." He confirmed it by remotely opening the trunk with his car key. He was so grateful that he could now drive home. But he needed a little help along the way.

STORY 8: REMEMBERING MY BROTHER COB

Carlos "Cob" Sheffield in 1989

I grew up in the segregated south in the 1940-50s. Even as a young farm kid, I never understood the reasoning for segregation based on the color of one's skin. Ruben was a black teenager who would work hard with us in the fields all day but at the noon break he could not eat at our kitchen table because, as Mom explained, "They'll chase us out of the county if we do." So, my younger brother Melvin and I would get our plates and eat on the back porch with Ruben.

During my teen years, my older brother, Cob, would let me help him do odd jobs for his plumbing business in Ft Meade, Florida. We did several plumbing jobs in Ft Meade's racially segregated "quarters" where black families lived. There were a couple of families living there who were having a rough time making it, so Cob would take them squirrels and rabbits that we had hunted on our farm. We always dressed the animal but left the feet on the carcass for the recipient to confirm that it was a rabbit or a squirrel.

In 2010, I met the owner of a new restaurant in Fort Meade. After a short conversation, we discovered that in June 1968 we had both been stationed in the same platoon at Army Paratrooper Training (Jump School) at Fort Benning, Georgia. He was about 18 years old at the time. At age 28, I had been the "old man" and the only Air Force officer in the Army platoon, so I did not get to know him. Now 42 years later, he told me a story about how our paths had crossed as children. He said that as a small child he often went hungry, and he told me how much his family appreciated my brother Cob bringing them free rabbits and squirrels. Although I was a teenager at the time of the delivery, I still had a vivid memory of a small boy standing behind the screen door watching while his mother came out to the plumbing truck to accept the "catch of the day."

Even though that child's early opportunities were limited, he had joined the Army, learned a profession, brought his family out of poverty, and now owned a successful restaurant business. All he needed was a little help along the way.

BLANK PAGES ARE PROVIDED FOR YOUR
ADDITIONAL FAMILY INFORMATION